essential Musicianship
for band
masterwork studies

B♭ trumpet

Paula Crider
Jack Saunders

ISBN-13: 978-0-634-08865-0
ISBN-10: 0-634-08865-3

HAL•LEONARD®
CORPORATION
7777 W. BLUEMOUND RD. P.O. BOX 13819 MILWAUKEE, WI 53213

Introduction...

Welcome to *Essential Musicianship for Band* and *Masterworks Studies*.

This student book contains many features designed to enrich your experience in band. You will be introduced to 6 classic works for band, the composers, as well as music history and culture. With the included CD-rom discs, Masterwork Studies also offers you some new ways to develop your music skills with recordings, and software tools for practice, creative activities, and self-assessment.

Through the study of high quality literature, you will develop overall musicianship, performance skills, and understanding of the art of music—accomplishments that will contribute to your success as a vital member of your band program.

Your Book Includes:

- Music excerpts, etudes, and special exercises for 6 classic works for band, to be used in conjunction with the full performance editions
- Full recordings of each work (CD-rom 1)
- Basics of Musicianship – important concepts that apply to all ensemble performance
- Practice loops with tempo adjustment software – for key sections of the Masterworks Studies, for technical and stylistic practice (CD-rom 1)
- Practice Guidelines – helpful tips for getting the most out of your practice sessions
- Web Connection – *www.halleonard.com/EMband* – a site for Masterwork Studies users, with more music, notation files, and templates, links to composer and other related sites, and more
- Vocabulary of music terms and techniques (back of book), coded in **boldface** throughout the book
- Scale and arpeggio studies in several major and minor keys
- SmartMusic® software (CD-rom 2). This special version gives you a practice and recording system for use with a computer. You can:
  - Practice the included technique studies in all keys with accompaniment
  - Record, save, and e-mail a performance (requires an external microphone) – with technique study accompaniments or a solo performance (no accompaniment)
  - Use the assessment system to check note and rhythm accuracy
  - Check fingerings for any note
  - Use the included metronome and electronic tuner
- Finale NotePad® software (CD-rom 2). This computer music application introduces the basics of music notation.
  - Quick set-up for any combination of instruments
  - Simple note and rhythm entry
  - Music playback (with computer sound card)
  - Print and e-mail a file
  - Reads and plays Finale® (full version) files
  - Free upgrades on web site

Installation instructions

To install SmartMusic® and Finale NotePad®, insert your CD-rom 2 into a PC or Mac computer and start the file, "Run me." Follow the on-screen instructions to complete the installation. Instructions and tutorials are located in the menu help files.

For practice loops with tempo adjustment software (Amazing Slow Downer), insert CD-rom 1 into a PC or Mac computer. Locate and start the Amazing Slow Downer application. Select a practice loop by track number (see guide below) and click the PLAY button. Use the slider bar to adjust to the desired tempo. For further instructions and key commands, consult the included menu help file.

Special note: SmartMusic® and NotePad® do not need a subscription to access the Essential Musicianship features. For SmartMusic®, always choose "Sample" to run the program, and for NotePad®, always choose "Remind Me Later."

CD-ROM 1 *For CD Player/Computer with CD-rom*

Track	Title	Track	Title
	First Suite in E♭		*English Folk Song Suite*
1	I Chaconne	20	Mvt. I 5–17
2	II Intermezzo	21	Mvt. I 65–80
3	III March	22	Mvt. II 43–58
		23	Mvt. III 89–113
	English Folk Song Suite		
4	I March		*Suite of Old American Dances*
5	II Intermezzo	24	Mvt. I 1–4
6	III March	25	Mvt. I 22–27
		26	Mvt. II 1–8
7	*Ye Banks and Braes O'Bonnie Doon*	27	Mvt. II 12–15
	Suite of Old American Dances	28	Mvt. IV 25–29
8	I Cake Walk	29	Mvt. V Rhy. 4/4
9	II Schottische	30	Mvt. V Rhy. 2/2
10	III Western One-Step	31	Mvt. V 17–20
11	IV Wallflower Waltz		
12	V Rag		*Overture to Candide*
		32	mm. 10–19
13	*Overture to Candide*	33	mm. 123–134
		34	mm. 190–201
14	*Incantation and Dance*	35	mm. 231–254

Practice Loops

Track	Title	Track	Title
	First Suite in E♭		*Incantation and Dance*
15	Mvt. I 39–49	36	mm. 70–76
16	Mvt. I 49–57	37	mm. 115–121
17	Mvt. II 83–91	38	mm. 187–193
18	Mvt. III 4–12	39	B♭ Tuning Notes
19	Mvt. III 13–28		

- Tempo Adjustment Software (CD-rom)

CD-ROM 2 *For Computer with CD-rom*

- SmartMusic® Software
- Finale NotePad® Software
- Essential Musicianship Data Files
  - NotePad® music files
- PDF files for printing
  - English Folksongs
  - Concert Etiquette
  - Manuscript Paper

The Basics of Ensemble Musicianship

What is musicianship?

Musicianship may be defined as the essence of artistic and highly skilled musical expression. Like other art forms, expression in music requires a set of skills that allows the artistry to flourish. Like a painter who develops and perfects techniques with paint, color, and textures, or a writer who uses various literary devices to create a dramatic scene, the art of music also requires basic skills that underlie the physical aspects of composing, performing, or conducting a musical work.

In an ensemble such as band or orchestra, musicianship is even larger in scope, as the musical experience is created with the talents of many individuals, who bring together their collective skills to create a unified, meaningful performance.

The basic elements of ensemble musicianship are listed below. Each element is an essential building block for learning and performing, and provides keys to fully enjoying your experience in band.

Playing in an Ensemble

It should be considered an honor to be a part of a musical ensemble. With that special membership, however, comes the responsibility to make worthwhile contributions to the ensemble. Through personal growth as a player and as an active participant in the artistic performance of the music, band members may enjoy the full rewards of ensemble musicianship.

Students should prepare for rehearsal just as they would for any other class. Learning the notes and rhythms outside of class time is one of the basic responsibilities of being an ensemble member. This allows valuable rehearsal time to be spent on the task at hand— the blending of all the individual parts into a successful, musical experience.

Before every rehearsal begins, you should:
- Make the choice to bring a positive attitude to rehearsal.
- Prepare the notes and rhythms outside of class.
- Be responsible for your instrument's playing condition.
- Have your music, a pencil, and other required materials.
- Warm-up appropriately.

Remember: Successful ensembles are built on "we," not "me."

Tone Quality

Since the overall quality of a band's sound is the sum of all the individual sounds, good ensemble musicianship includes playing with the best possible tone quality—every player in the band.

The characteristic sound of an instrument is what makes it unique and recognizable. This sound, or tone quality, is generally described in terms of resonance and focus. The best sounds are usually depicted as rich, full, and sonorous, allowing them to blend well with other ensemble sounds. Experienced players who produce a characteristic tone quality often think of moving the air stream through their instruments, rather than merely into it.

To improve your tone quality and the characteristic sound of your instrument:

- Listen to recordings of renowned artists on your instrument or instrument family.
- Ask your director, private teacher, or a professional player to help you develop a characteristic tone quality, learning from their ideas, techniques and practical advice.
- Use the best possible instrument available to you.
- Make sure your instrument is in perfect working order.
- Learn about the physics of sound and how it works with your instrument.
- Practice simple music exercises that allow you to focus just on tone quality.
- Record yourself and listen back critically; good players constantly make judgments and adjustments to improve their tone quality.

Remember: Total Ensemble Sound = Sum of All Individual Tone Qualities

Intonation

Most performers think of good intonation, or the art of "playing in tune," as one of the most critical aspects of good ensemble musicianship. Like tone quality, each ensemble player's sense of pitch is multiplied many times, and has a profound effect on the entire group's performance.

For experienced players, intonation is a constant point of focus. To begin, a good player ensures his/her instrument is "matched" to the pitch source, then constantly makes adjustments during rehearsal and performance, sometimes on every note of a passage. This practice involves careful listening to locate the pitch center within the ensemble, and is followed by subtle changes with air and embouchure.

Helpful tips to improve intonation:

- For most instruments, tuning to concert B♭ is a good starting point, but does not ensure that all other notes are in tune. Just playing notes with correct fingerings and air support does not guarantee pitch accuracy on all notes.
- All instruments are different, but many have "tendencies" that can be realized and then adjusted. (Example: without adjustment, low concert C on trumpet is usually sharp).
- Develop your critical listening skills. You must be able to hear pitch problems before you can correct them. Learn to listen for acoustic "beats," and adjust the pitch up or down until they are eliminated.
- Focus on intonation in your own practice sessions, without the distraction of other players.
- Learn how your instrument responds and how you can adjust it on specific notes and problematic registers (high and low ranges). Make an intonation graph to chart your instrument's tendencies.
- Electronic tuners can be helpful in learning the pitch tendencies on your instrument.
- Be aware that your instrument's pitch can constantly change because of temperature. The pitch rises (becomes more sharp) as temperature increases, and lowers (becomes flatter) in colder temperatures. Also, your physical playing habits (i.e. fatigue) and your level of listening affect your instrument's pitch.
- No one tuning pitch is ideal for all instruments. Combinations of various notes, such as concert F, G, A, and B♭, may help the tuning process.
- Learn alternate fingerings/slide positions for intonation adjustments.
- Generally, woodwinds (except flute) tend to go flat on crescendos and brasses tend to go sharp.

Remember: Along with tone quality, good intonation from all players is a critical building block of a rich ensemble sound. Just like professional orchestras and bands, great performances come from those groups who are constantly focused on intonation.

Breathing and Breath Support

How a musician breathes has the most significant impact on tone quality and intonation. Good air control and air manipulation techniques are critical and are often more challenging than it would seem. Air control requires good posture, proper air intake, and a well-supported breath release.

Good posture means:
- Feet flat on the floor
- Sitting upright near the front of the chair
- Sitting tall to allow the air to move freely
- A sense of overall relaxation, without stiffness

The air intake process brings the air into the lungs in preparation for tone production. This includes:
- Breathing in through the mouth
- Keeping the throat open as if inhaling the syllable "ohh"
- Breathing "in tempo" with the musical pulse (slow tempos = long breaths)
- Breathing deeply, evidenced by expanding around the waistline
- Shoulders staying down and relaxed

A well-supported release of air moves the air from the lungs through the instrument and creates the tone. This is accomplished by:
- Pushing the air upward by exerting the intercostal muscles down and outward
- Putting speed and pressure behind the air stream
- Releasing the air steadily and at the required pace

Final thought: Development of good breathing technique must be practiced diligently until each step becomes a natural part of one's playing.

Ensemble Balance

One of the unique traits of a concert band sound, or "sonority," is its special combination of wind instruments, accompanied by the percussion section. This combination, with its various instrument colors, or timbres, is what defines a true band sound.

The best chordal balance and blend for most band compositions is based on a simple concept—most of the sound should come from the lowest instruments and decrease in quantity, or level, as we move upward. Since higher instruments naturally project more easily, less sound is needed from them.

The following chart, or "pyramid," illustrates this concept. Notice how fewer instruments or their level of sound is needed at the top of the pyramid.

If too many upper instruments are playing at levels that reverse this concept, then an unstable sound results – one that lacks sonority and richness.

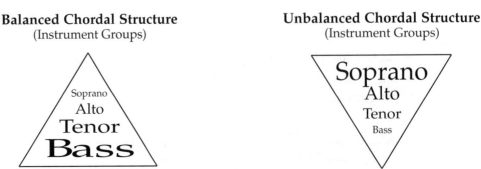

Balanced Chordal Structure
(Instrument Groups)

Unbalanced Chordal Structure
(Instrument Groups)

While you cannot directly affect the number of players assigned to the various parts, it is important to know your role in the overall sound picture. Many experienced players who play treble clef or upper range instruments use a technique known as "listening down" to help them find their proper place in the band's sonority.

Voice Priority

A closely related concept to ensemble balance is voice priority, or the relative importance of individual parts (voices) in the overall sound of a musical composition.

To create interest and variety, composers create many combinations of music structures, through orchestration and musical techniques. As a player in that framework, you should always be aware of your own part's purpose and priority in the music texture.

Below is a general guide that may be applied to many music settings. Any combination of these "voices" may be considered.

Voice Priority Guide

Importance	Part/Line (Voice)
1	Melody
2	Countermelody
3	Rhythmic accompaniment
4	Sustained accompaniment

It is common for these combinations to change from section to section in a piece of music, sometimes very quickly. If players realize how their parts fit into the total sound picture, and adjust their dynamics, style and intensity, the correct overall balance will be much easier to achieve.

Dynamics

The use of dynamics is an important tool for composers to create emotional impact and musical interest in a piece. For performers in an ensemble, the dynamic possibilities go far beyond the two basic levels of "loud" and "soft". Ensemble playing requires skill at all levels. Because of the air control and resonance needed, particularly p and pp, it is challenging for wind players to play at various dynamic levels, while maintaining good tone quality and intonation. Soft dynamics still require fast air, but the volume of air is reduced.

Also, for balance and texture refinements, it is important for ensemble members to agree on the basic dynamic levels. To gain a sense of the various levels, one may think of *mezzo forte* (*mf*) as being 50% of total volume. All other dynamics may then be viewed in proportion to *mezzo forte*.

Dynamic Levels
(Percentage of total volume)

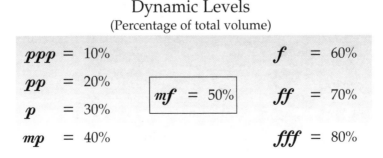

To develop each of the levels, practice scales by playing the first note at 10% and each subsequent note at the next dynamic or percentage. Also, begin at 80% and decreasing the volume as the scale ascends or descends. This requires concentration and control but can develop the aural, mental and physical skill needed for playing at all dynamic levels.

Articulation and Style

A key element of music performance is musical style, e.g., the distinctive character or genre of a work or passage. Many times the melody, harmony, rhythm, or tempo determine the musical style; however, the nuances within these frameworks are created with various articulation marks.

Unfortunately, composers, publishers, and conductors have used a wide variety of markings and interpretations, often creating confusion. Experienced players have learned to adapt the written part to the musical context, the judgment of the conductor, or most importantly, to their own sensible music tastes. Here is a description of the four basic articulation markings and their most common usage:

A **staccato** mark indicates a shortened, yet resonant sound, usually in music textures that depict lightness, but also with separation between notes. A common fault for players is to "clip" staccato notes, thus cutting off their resonance and sense of direction. Think of these light notes as full sounding, but shorter than normal.

Tenuto markings most often indicate a full value note, as opposed to notes that are shortened and separated. The effect is intended to create a smooth, connected sound by using softer, less explosive syllables (DU). Tenuto notes are sometimes used in conjunction with the style term "legato."

An **accent** indicates emphasis with more volume or air pressure at the beginning of the sound with a rapid taper. Many times, accented notes are mistakenly separated, rather than played with full value. Some certain styles and tempi, such as a march, do require that accented notes are both emphasized and separated.

A **marcato accent** (sometimes called a "sforzando accent," "rooftop,"cap," or "hammer") indicates the strongest accent or emphasis, with even more force than the > mark. Classical composers used this mark on all note values, long and short, whereas contemporary writers tend to use it to indicate both a hard attack and a shortened note value that does not have the rapid taper of the accent.

Unmarked passages also create stylistic confusion in an ensemble setting. As a rule, notes with no markings or slurs should be played with standard tonguing (the syllable "TU"), being careful to choose a note length that fits the general style and tempo.

Remember, the overall character of the music, usually determined by the conductor, defines how articulation marks are to be played. Because so many variations exist, a good musician needs to have an understanding of each marking's possibilities, and then adapt and interpret them correctly.

Ensemble Precision

Rhythmic and technical precision in an ensemble creates a listening atmosphere that brings excitement, nuance, and added drama to a musical style. Ensemble precision should not be limited to music that is note-intensive, up-tempo, and technically demanding. It can also apply to the most sensitive of textures, where simple musical ideas need careful, proper execution to achieve the full, expressive effect.

Your best contribution as a player is dependent on the proper techniques for rhythmic accuracy and clarity, and appropriate note releases (and attacks). To enhance your contribution to the ensemble, here are some suggestions to building rhythmic precision and technical facility (also review Practice Guidelines chapter).

For practice sessions:
- Use a metronome to develop evenness in your playing.
- Develop a counting system to understand patterns and subdivisions.
- Mark in beats and subdivisions in pencil.
- Practice difficult rhythms first on a single pitch.
- Simplify or remove the articulation until the notes are mastered.
- Start with small, short figures, then add notes and groups of notes.
- Use clapping and singing approaches.
- Practice passages backwards to explore every learning angle.
- Avoid emphasis on tempo; strive for accuracy and evenness before speed.

To master technical execution with clarity, each performer must understand that note weights lighten as they become shorter. In similar fashion, as note lengths become shorter (or faster), the style of articulation should also become lighter.

Remember: If you plan to travel quickly, travel lightly!

Attacks (initiation of tone)
- Always memorize the first measure of an entrance so that you may watch your conductor.
- Breathe in tempo.
- Explore various syllables so the attack (tone initiation) will better reflect the required style ("doo" for legato, "toh" for fat staccato, "tih" for shorter staccato, "tah" for accents, "dah" for more emphasis).

Note releases
The ending of musical sounds (release) is equally as important as the start of the sound (attack). Keep in mind:
- A note followed by rest is most accurately released into the rest.
- Stopping on the last count of a note usually "cheats" the correct note length.
- Releases are best accomplished by gradually elevating the tongue as the air supply is compressed and diminished.
- Avoid placing the tip of the tongue against the reed or mouthpiece to stop the air.
- Think in terms of lifting and rounding the sounds to help taper releases.
- Notes at phrase endings usually require a conscious effort to play a full note value, before a rapid breath is taken to continue.

Interpretation

Most teachers and students agree that the most difficult skill to teach or learn is music interpretation. How the printed characters translate into an artistic performance is indeed very subjective, and in most situations, there is no clear cut approach that surpasses all others.

Students should be encouraged to be expressive and to evaluate the interpretive suggestions set forth by their sections and their director. It is important to understand that music is not a static, immobile art form, but rather that it is a dramatic, emotional force that is either moving forward to a point of arrival, or is moving away from that point to build anew. Knowledge of performance traditions, musical taste, sensitivity, and imagination can be important guides in the interpretive process of making great music come to life.

Here are some general guidelines for music interpretation:

- Music never remains static. It moves toward a climax (crescendo) or away from one (decrescendo).
- Pickup notes in a slower, lyric style may be played with a "stretching" or tenuto feel.
- Always look for the high point in a musical phrase, then play with enough contrast to build to that point and move away.
- Add motion to melodic sequences (repetitive-type figures) by adding cresc./decresc. nuances.
- Repeated note or rhythm patterns should crescendo to an arrival point, usually a longer note value.

Final thoughts on interpretation and musical expression

Music, by its very nature, is a personal vehicle of expression. However, in an ensemble, the art of interpretation becomes a collaborative effort, one that reflects the talents, skills, and artistry of all the participants.

For many musicians, the thrill of a great performance in an ensemble is one of the most satisfying experiences of all. With the challenges, encouragement, success, and common bond they share with fellow players, the expression of music, as created by the entire ensemble, becomes everyone's greatest reward.

Practice Guidelines

Practice. Practice. Practice.

Have you ever felt a rush of confidence and pride following a flawless performance on your instrument? Conversely, have you ever experienced the unsettling sense of self-doubt that said, "I can't do this," when you were not fully prepared to perform?

Practice yields confidence and confidence yields success. Through regular practice, students may develop a beautiful tone quality, perform with improved style and intonation, increase range and flexibility, master complex technical demands, and acquire greater skill in expressive playing and dynamic control. Practice requires discipline and determination, and the reward will be the thrill of high achievement. Below are some guidelines for establishing and maintaining a regular practice routine.

The Set-Up

A Place to Practice
- Find a quiet space that minimizes distractions.
- Use a standard music stand. An improvised stand may cause poor posture.
- Stand while practicing, or sit in a solid chair. Exhibit good posture at all times.

Recommended Equipment
The following accessories and equipment are excellent aids for practice.
- metronome (strongly recommended)
- pencil
- mirror (use to check embouchure/posture/hand position)
- practice chart (to set goals, record and measure progress)
- recording device (to assess performance)
- computer/CD-rom (for practice tracks, assessment, and modeling)

Daily Practice Schedule

Set aside a specific time each day for practice. The length of the practice session is dependent upon your endurance level. Practice sessions should become longer as you become a stronger player. It is recommended that you devote at least one hour of consistent, sustained practice each day with one day per week for rest.

Practice Routine

Practice sessions yield the best results when they are structured. The following suggested practice routine provides a basic design for daily use:

Warm-up
Just as great athletes would never attempt demanding physical exercise without proper warm-up, musicians should also warm up the muscles before exposing them to the stress of performance. If subjected to inordinate stress without proper warm-up, a muscle may actually be damaged.

The key to a proper warm-up is to begin with slow extended sounds in the middle register of the instrument at a comfortable (*mf*) volume. A good warm-up routine might include long tones, lip slurs (brass), harmonics (woodwinds), slow scales, thirds and arpeggios, and instrument-specific exercises.

Exercises
Scales, thirds, chromatics and arpeggios should be included in every practice session. Other exercises in this category might include long tones, etudes, rhythmic studies, style/articulation exercises, tonguing exercises, studies for range and dynamic control, increasing technical facility and so forth. The metronome is a useful tool during this time.

Musical Excerpts and Repertoire
The purpose of this portion of the practice session is to focus on your performance music, such as solos, ensembles, band music and so forth. Isolate problem measures and practice slowly until each aspect is accurate, then gradually increase speed. Take larger sections of the music and repeat the same process.

A Favorite Piece
End your practice session by playing something that you truly enjoy playing. Memorize these favorites so that you may close your eyes and enjoy what you hear.

Six Hints for Success

1. Don't practice your mistakes.
Practicing a difficult technical passage at a tempo that is faster than your technical ability only compounds the problem; you are simply practicing your mistakes. To avoid this, begin a challenging section in slow motion, practicing at perhaps half the written tempo. Allow each note to speak. Then gradually increase the speed. (A metronome is a very useful practice tool.)

2. Focus on one aspect at a time.
If you're having trouble with rhythm, play the entire passage on one note and focus on the rhythm only. On the other hand, if developing a better tone is a priority, then use one note as a base of departure. If you can play 80% of the piece well, isolate and practice only the problem measures. Soon you will be able to play the entire piece well.

3. Take it slow.
Slow practice is the key to success. Why does slow practice make faster passages easier? As musicians, we rely upon muscle memory for accurate performance. Muscle memory is strengthened through repetition—accurate repetition. Each time you repeat an activity in exactly the same manner, a neural path is formed in the brain. This synaptic response becomes stronger and stronger until it is ingrained and it becomes a habit. To perform with a high degree of accuracy, these neural paths must become well-traveled territory.

4. Ten times in a row (TTAR).
This is a proven method for developing accuracy. Select one measure or phrase and play it once correctly. Then, go back and play it twice correctly; then three times, and so forth until you attain ten correct performances. If you play the measure correctly four times, but on the fifth time a note is missed, then you must go back to beginning and start all over again. You may want to begin with the goal twice in a row on one day, three times in a row the next day, and continue each day until the goal of ten times in a row is achieved.

5. Use a metronome.
A metronome is an invaluable tool. It can also be beneficial to monitor your progress by keeping a metronome chart (see below). Write down your beginning tempo. Practice at this tempo until the excerpt is mastered. Increase the tempo to the next metronomic marking. Repeat the process. You may want to begin each practice at the preceding day's marking, and increase the tempo as you are able.

Sample Metronome Chart

Date	Excerpt	Tempo
9/16	HOLST Eb MM. 105–114	76
9/17	"	84
9/18	"	86

Note: You may also pencil in the metronome markings in your music to indicate your progress.

6. Progressive Practice
Practice sessions should be based on long-term and short-term goals. A short-term goal might be to increase the tempo of a technical exercise by 12 metronomic beats in a week. A long-term goal might be to increase your playing range by three notes, or to increase your tonguing speed by 20 metronomic beats. It has been found that students who establish both long-term and short-term goals quickly discover the rewards of progressive practice.

Overcoming Problem Areas

Tone Quality

Without a beautiful tone, all the dazzling technique in the world is worthless.

- A beautiful, sonorous, characteristic tone is dependent upon air, embouchure and equipment, but most of all it is dependent upon CONCEPT. Before any student musician can produce a rich and resonant tone, he/she must have a clear idea of how he/she wants the instrument to sound in the "mind's ear." Review the suggestions for tone quality in the section of this book titled "Basics of Ensemble Musicianship."
- Listening to a few minutes of your favorite brass, woodwind or percussion soloist immediately prior to a practice session will serve to provide an excellent "tone model" for the session.

Rhythmic Accuracy

- Separate technique from rhythm by playing the passage on one note.
- Subdivide to the next divisible pulse. (For example, when playing quarter notes, mentally subdivide to 8th notes.)
- Approach a challenging measure much as you might a math problem. Break the problem rhythms down and pencil in the counts with upbeats and downbeats.
- Clap and sing the rhythm.
- Practice rhythmic exercises to aid in pattern recognition.
- Do not be afraid to ask for help!

Breath Support

- Sit or stand tall with good posture.
- Sit away from the back of the chair so that your lungs are not restricted.
- Think of "inhaling a basketball and expelling a thread."
- Play a long, slurred passage at a prescribed tempo until you run out of air. Repeat the process and add a note each time you perform.
- Play a long tone while observing a second hand on a watch or clock. Keep a chart of your progress.

Technical Facility

- Practice with a metronome.
- Begin slowly, and gradually increase your speed.
- Alter articulation and rhythmic patterns. (♬♬ to ♪♩ to ♫.)
- Play one note, then play two notes, then add another, and so forth.
- Play the passage backwards.
- Memorize the problem passage.

Suggestions for Performance Success

- Take a few deep, calming breaths to reduce performance anxiety.
- Don't focus on what may have gone wrong; rather, look ahead and make the rest even better.
- Be "in the zone." Focus on nothing but the music.
- Enjoy yourself. Even with intensity, showing your enthusiasm in performance has a profound effect on the audience. *"Your heart is on fire while your mind is on ice."*

Composer Profile

Gustav Holst
(1874–1934)

"Teaching of art is itself an art ... we who are teachers should hold up our heads more proudly. We are among the lucky ones of the earth. If we are real artists in teaching, we have the greatest joy this world can give—that of creative work." [1]

– Gustav Holst

Gustav Holst is celebrated both as a passionate music educator and a distinguished 20th-century composer. He is best remembered for his orchestral composition, *The Planets*. Born in Cheltenham, England, on September 21, 1874, Holst had a difficult childhood. He suffered with chronic asthma, severe nearsightedness, and a crippling inflammation of the nerves in his right hand, which lasted throughout his life. Despite these problems, Holst's father, a pianist, organist and choirmaster, taught him piano lessons. His mother, a singer, died when he was only 8. Holst also studied the violin and trombone with the hope that the latter would strengthen his ailing lungs. An extremely musical child, Holst began to compose music at the age of 12.

Nearly penniless at age 21, Holst won a composition scholarship to the Royal College of Music. He studied with two of the most reputable teachers of the day, Stanford and Parry, and it was there that he met Ralph Vaughan Williams. Holst and Vaughan Williams met weekly to study and analyze each other's compositions, and became lifelong friends.

In the summers, Holst supplemented his income by playing trombone in bands at various seaside resorts, and ultimately became proficient enough to secure a professional position in the Carl Rosa Opera Company. These experiences played an important role in Holst's development as a skilled writer for wind and orchestral groups.

Holst's inquisitive nature led to his interest in Eastern culture. He learned to translate Sanskrit so he could better understand Hindu philosophy. In 1905, Ralph Vaughan Williams recommended Holst to become his replacement as Musical Director at the St. Paul's Girls School in London, a position Holst held until his death. Holst later accepted a position at the Morley College for Working Men and Women and taught night classes there for many years.

In 1913, a new music wing was built at St. Paul's School and Holst was given a large, soundproof office in which to teach private lessons, and compose music. He later remarked that his two most prized possessions at that time were the key to this office, and Beethoven's tuning fork, a gift from an admiring, fellow music-lover.

At one point during his teaching career, Holst held four separate

[1] Vaughan Williams, Ursula, ed., and Holst, Imogen, ed., *Heirs and Rebels: Letters to Each Other and Occasional Writings by Gustav Holst and Ralph Vaughan Williams.* Oxford: Oxford University Press, 1959. pp. 66–73.

Gustav von * *Holst*

Soundproof office at St. Paul's

teaching positions. His correspondence indicates that he was a dedicated and inspiring teacher. Holst related that one of his high points occurred when he arrived at his classroom early one morning, and discovered some of his students already there, singing Palestrina "for the sheer love of music."[2]

The Planets elevated Holst to the pinnacle of his profession and became so popular that over 75 performances were presented in the United Kingdom during the six years following World War I. In spite of his success, Holst was described as a shy and unassuming man. He refused all honorary awards and degrees, credited others for the success of his works, and refused to grant newspaper interviews. Although reserved, Holst displayed a great sense of humor. Vaughan Williams believed that had Holst not chosen music as a career, he could have become a successful comedian.

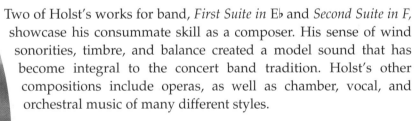

Two of Holst's works for band, *First Suite in E♭* and *Second Suite in F*, showcase his consummate skill as a composer. His sense of wind sonorities, timbre, and balance created a model sound that has become integral to the concert band tradition. Holst's other compositions include operas, as well as chamber, vocal, and orchestral music of many different styles.

Holst's ashes are buried in Chichester Cathedral near the grave of Renaissance composer Thomas Weelkes, who was the organist there more than 300 years before. Thanks to the work of his daughter, Imogen, much of Holst's music that might have been lost has been preserved.

* Holst changed his name, at the beginning of World War I, dropping "von."

[2] *The Christian Science Monitor,* 1942.

First Suite in E♭ for Military Band

Gustav Holst

Introduction to the Music

Gustav Holst wrote the *First Suite in E♭ for Military Band* in 1909. Little is known about the circumstances that compelled him to compose what has become known as the first master-work for band in the 20th century. It may have been written for a military band competition, for which the first prize of 50 guineas would have provided welcome income; or it could have been composed for the Royal Military School of Music at Kneller Hall, where the first documented performance did not take place until 1920.

Although the *First Suite* may be played by as few as 19 players and percussion, the Kneller Hall performance featured a 165-piece band! A review of this performance in a local news-paper stated: " ...yet, apart from such raggedness as you might expect from 40 boy-clarinets in **unison**, there was a breezy life in their performances."[1]

[1] Mitchell, Jon C. *Journal of Band Research.* Vol. 20, #1. Fall, 1984. p. 45.

Listening Experience

Mvt. I: Chaconne

Chaconne is based on an 8-bar **ground bass** initially stated by the baritone and tuba. Holst then presents 15 variations of the theme in various instrumental settings. For example, it is heard in the trombones in m. 8, solo horn at C, and upper woodwinds just after E. It is also heard in varied styles: a detached 8th-note version at B, followed by a chorale-like setting, and then **inverted** at letter D . This movement provides an excellent example of Holst's superb compositional skills.

Focus:

■ Observe the smooth, flowing style of the chaconne melody.
■ Notice the clarity of the **octave** tuning between the tuba and baritone.
■ Listen to the many ways Holst presents the 8-bar chaconne theme.

The form of this movement uses the theme and 15 variations based on:

Boldface vocabulary words, see pages 87–88

MM. 1–8 Chaconne Theme (Unison/Octave tuning)

Focus:

- Play with a clear, focused and beautiful tone quality.
- Listen carefully to the **unison** tuning within your section and to **octave** tuning between voices.
- The objective is to eliminate all "acoustic beats" from the sound.
- "Listen down" to the tuba line for pitch reference.
- Initiate the first tone with a gentle **legato** attack.
- Move smoothly and seamlessly between notes.
- Shape the **phrase** as your director suggests.
- The breath at m. 4 must be quick and the next note non-accented.

Special Technique…

"**Listen down**" – listen for the lowest notes in the ensemble sonority as a reference for pitch and balance. (Ex. – flutes and trumpets listen to the low brass to adjust their pitch and balance)

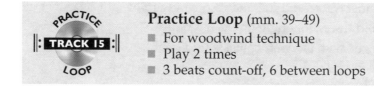

Practice Loop (mm. 39–49)
- For woodwind technique
- Play 2 times
- 3 beats count-off, 6 between loops

MM. 39–49 Music Excerpt

Focus:

- All voices *crescendo* to *ff* at B .
- Stress woodwind 16ths to correspond with brass 8th notes.
- 16th notes should employ fast air and relentless rhythmic precision.
- 8th notes should provide resonant punctuations and should not be too short.

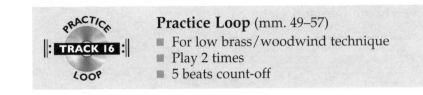

MM. 49–57 Music Excerpt

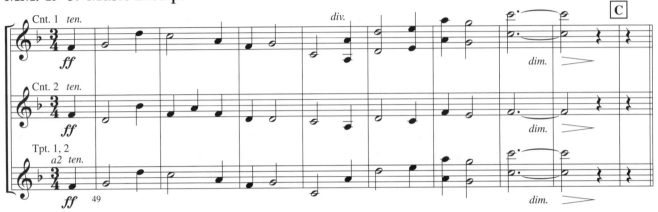

Focus:

- Balance the chorale and moving bass line so that neither part covers the other.
- Chaconne theme should be shaped as the opening section.
- The low brass/woodwind *pesante* style should be played in a slightly detached manner, yet sound full and resonant with weight on each tone.
- Avoid heavy tonguing on the 8th notes.
- Tongue with an open vowel sound (taah).

MM. 105–114 Music Excerpt

Focus:

- The chaconne theme must be played with massive and energized tone quality.
- Listen and adjust **octave** tuning.
- Balance upper woodwinds so that careful listening will produce good intonation.
- A crescendo will enhance the ascending **scale** at mm. 105–106.
- Sustained parts should stagger breathing.

Listening Experience

Mvt. II: Intermezzo

An **intermezzo** is traditionally used to connect the main divisions of a symphony, but Holst uses this light, energetic movement as a contrast to the somewhat somber mood of the *Chaconne*. Holst again presents the chaconne motive, this time in a faster rhythmic setting.

Motive from the Chaconne theme

Focus:

- Listen to the energy created by the **syncopation**.
- Notice the light, almost brittle **staccato** style.
- Observe the contrasting lyrical style at C.

MM. 1–17 Playing with Proper Style

Focus:

- The melodic 8th notes are short. Quarter and dotted quarter notes should be long and stressed.
- The rapid staccato accompaniment (line B) is short and dry.
- Balance the accompaniment to the melodic line.
- The accents bring this movement to life.
- Keep the tempo moving ahead. This movement must not drag or lose energy.

MM. 39–42 Music Excerpt (Crescendo and technical accuracy)

Focus:

- Move the printed crescendo back one measure and add *subito p*.
- Accompaniment 8th notes must not cover woodwind 16th notes.
- Woodwind 16th notes must begin with confidence and crescendo molto.
- Practice this section in slow motion, gradually accelerating.
- Listen for the "ring" of a well articulated staccato.

Practice Loop (mm. 83–91)
- For clarinet style/technique
- Play 2 times
- 4 beats count-off

MM. 83–91 Music Excerpt (Expressive phrasing)

Focus:

- Solo cornet/baritone parts must match in volume, intonation, and **timbre**, and must shape the **phrase**.
- The moving woodwind line must also add phrase shape, while not covering the melodic line.
- Whole notes should be played softly, with a sensitive ear given to the moving lines.
- The style is a singing **legato**, with consonant sounds used to articulate (D syllable).

Listening Experience

Mvt. III: March

Holst begins this movement with an **inversion** of the chaconne theme, and the original motive in the trio section (see example below). The march opens with a typical British brass band setting (e.g. without woodwinds). Holst includes "For Military Band" in the title as a means to distinguish between full band and brass band. (British brass bands are still quite popular in the United Kingdom and may be comprised of musicians ranging from teenagers to senior citizens. The very best of these bands compete in the annual National Brass Band Championships, an event well worth attending should the opportunity ever arise.)

The final movement of the *Suite in E♭* is filled with energy and should be performed in a typical British manner. The tempo is not as fast as the standard American march, and the style should project a stately, but energetic dignity.

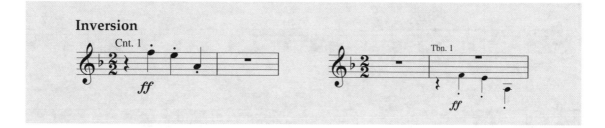

Inversion

Focus:

- Listen for the characteristic, detached march style.
- Notice how Holst skillfully brings both themes together at D.

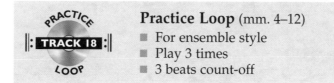

Practice Loop (mm. 4–12)
- For ensemble style
- Play 3 times
- 3 beats count-off

MM. 4–12 Unison Melody Study

Focus:

- "Sting" the 1st note (*ff*), then quickly *decresc.* to *f*.
- All quarter and 8th notes are **staccato** – light and short.
- Accented notes are long with a *f* attack and rapid diminuendo.
- Listen for precise, vertical rhythmic alignment.
- Use fast air and a light tongue on 8th notes.

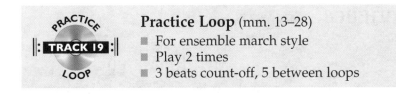

Practice Loop (mm. 13–28)
- For ensemble march style
- Play 2 times
- 3 beats count-off, 5 between loops

MM. 13–28 Music Excerpt (Proper March style)

Focus:
- Stress the accented dotted quarter notes.
- Slightly increase intensity on repeated figures.
- Use short, crisp articulation on staccato quarter notes.
- The moving line should be heard over static pitches.

MM. 71–88 Music Excerpt (Legato/staccato contrasts)

Focus:

- The lyric, slurred phrase requires dynamic shaping.
- Listen and adjust for good **unison/octave** tuning.
- Staccato quarter notes must be soft and lightly articulated, but with good tonal focus.

MM. 146–151 Music Excerpt (Balancing themes)

Focus:

- Balance parts so that both themes are clearly projected.
- Upper woodwind and high brass must maintain staccato articulation.
- Low brass half notes should be accented, but not separated.
- Quarter note at the end of the phrase must not be too short.

Creative Activities

- Research the differences in instrumentation between a British brass band and your school band.
- Listen to a recording of Holst's most famous orchestral composition, *The Planets*.
- Holst wrote *The Planets* in 1920, but the planet Pluto was not discovered until 1930. Compose a 16-measure movement to add to *The Planets*, titled "Pluto" (manuscript paper or NotePad® software).

Composer Profile

Ralph Vaughan Williams
(1872–1958)

Ralph Vaughan Williams is arguably one of the greatest British composers of the 20th century. Born at Down Ampney, Gloucestershire, England on October 12, 1872, Vaughan Williams' insatiable appetite for learning soon emerged. At age 4, he learned to read, and at age 6 he wrote his first composition, a four-bar piece entitled *The Robin's Nest*. His father died when Ralph was barely 2 years old. His mother, Margaret, took her three children to live with her parents at Leith Hill Place, a family estate with 12 servants.

Ralph (pronounced "Rafe," rhymes with "safe") enjoyed a carefree childhood. His Aunt Sophie gave him his first piano lessons, and taught him music theory. He delighted in his toy theater, composing overtures to plays acted out by his toy dogs. At age 8, Vaughan Williams enrolled in a music composition correspondence course offered by the University of Edinburgh. At age 11, he was sent to Field House School, where his mischievous nature reportedly got him into trouble. Vaughan Williams played his violin after hours "which set the boys dancing in their shirts and the master came in."[1] He later switched to the viola, and expressed a desire to become a professional violist, but his family discouraged this pursuit, claiming it was "beneath his station."

Vaughan Williams' education was impressive. He received a comprehensive academic education at Charterhouse and Trinity College in Cambridge. Vaughan Williams then attended the Royal College, where he studied with Stanford and Parry, two of the most prominent teachers of that generation. It was at the Royal College of Music where Vaughan Williams met composer Gustav Holst, who became his lifelong friend. The two composers often met to discuss and critique one another's compositions, and Vaughan Williams claimed that Holst was "the greatest influence on my music…"[2]

[1] Morre, Jerrold Northrop. *Vaughan Williams, A Life In Photographs.* New York: Oxford University Press, 1992. p. 24.

[2] *Ibid.*, p. 26.

With friend Gustav Holst

In 1904, Vaughan Williams became a member of the Folk Song Society, and developed a passion for collecting and preserving songs sung by the English peasantry - songs that would otherwise have been lost. It was his love of these English folk songs that inspired Vaughan Williams to compose ambitious, new musical works. Among them, *Fantasia on a Theme by Thomas Tallis*, remains one of his most frequently performed pieces.

At the outbreak of World War I, Vaughan Williams enlisted in the Royal Army Medical Corps. There he spent three years scrubbing hospital floors and serving on night detail as a stretcher-bearer. He then transferred to an artillery squadron in France, where constant exposure to the sound of large guns contributed to an increasing deafness in his later years. In 1939, Great Britain entered World War II. Vaughan Williams was too old to enlist, so he contributed to the war effort by scoring the soundtrack for the movie *49th Parallel*. Another of Vaughan Williams' film scores, composed for *Scott of the Antarctic*, was later reworked into what would eventually become his *Antarctic Symphony*.

Ralph Vaughan Williams' compositional career spanned an incredible 65 years. His works for band are among the cornerstones of 20th century concert band repertoire: *Sea Songs*, *Toccata Marziale*, *Flourish for Wind Band*, *Rhosymedre* (arr. Beeler), *Henry the Fifth*, *The Golden Vanity* (unpublished), and *English Folk Song Suite*. His *Concerto for Oboe* and *Concerto for Tuba* are compelling musical studies for advanced players of those instruments. Vaughan Williams' other compositions include: nine symphonies, 11 film scores, numerous choral works, an opera, and a piano concerto.

After a lifetime of serving as a champion of British culture, Ralph Vaughan Williams died in 1958 at age 85. He leaves a legacy of music filled with patriotic pride and artistic passion. Vaughan Williams' ashes are buried in Westminster Abbey, alongside England's greatest artists and poets.

English Folk Song Suite

Ralph Vaughan Williams

Introduction to the Music

"Folk music is the foundation on which all our art music must rest."– Ralph Vaughan Williams

English Folk Song Suite was written for the Royal Military School of Music at Kneller Hall, London, England, and first performed on July 4, 1923. The piece was written at the request of Colonel Sommerville, Commandant of Kneller Hall.

Vaughan Williams' wife, Ursula wrote: "This [*English Folk Song Suite*] had been one of the works he had been particularly happy to undertake, as he enjoyed working in a medium new to him. A military band was a change from an orchestra, and in his not-so-far-off army days, [he felt] that a chance to play real tunes would be an agreeable and salutary experience for bandsmen."[1] (In Great Britain, the term "military band" is used to denote a band comprised of brass, woodwinds and percussion, as opposed to the popular British "brass band," which uses no woodwinds.)

As it was with his fellow composers Percy Grainger and Gustav Holst, Vaughan Williams became an avid collector of English folksongs. It was his wish to preserve these songs which had been sung for many generations, but had never been written down. The beginning of the 20th century marked the onset of the industrial revolution. Many rural farmers moved to the cities to seek employment, and the folksong tradition of these "country folk" was rapidly being lost.

Were it not for the passion of Vaughan Williams and other folksong collectors, these wonderfully tuneful songs might have been lost forever. Vaughan Williams enjoyed "rambles" (long walks) through the rural English countryside. It was not unusual to find him and his lifelong friend Gustav Holst taking a 40- or 50-mile hike, pen and manuscript paper in hand, stopping to chat with area locals in hopes of coaxing from them a folksong or two. Vaughan Williams collected over 800 folksongs; the last was collected only three years prior to his death in 1958.

English Folk Song Suite, in three movements, is based upon the following folksongs:

   Mvt. I : "Seventeen Come Sunday," "Pretty Caroline," "Dives and Lazarus"

   Mvt. II: "My Bonny Boy," "Green Bushes"

   Mvt. III: "Blow Away the Morning Dew," "High Germany," "Whistle, Daughter, Whistle," "John Barleycorn"

English Folk Song Suite is a solid example of the **nationalism** that was prevalent in England, especially between the two World Wars. Vaughan Williams frequently uses **modes** rather than major or minor **scales** to accurately represent the English folk melodies. The **Dorian scale** on F is the most frequently utilized mode in the *Folk Song Suite*. The C **Aeolian scale** appears in the third movement.

Along with the Holst Suites in E♭ and F, this was one of the first works of the 20th century specifically composed for the wind band. With its tuneful melodies, skillful scoring, and innovative **polymetric** combining of themes, Vaughan Williams' compositional genius has provided bands with a work of lasting significance.

---

[1] Vaughan Williams, Ursula. *R.V.W.: A Biography of Ralph Vaughan Williams.* London: Oxford University Press, 1964. p. 151.

Boldface vocabulary words, see pages 87–88

Listening Experience

Mvt. I: March – "Seventeen Come Sunday"

Focus:

- Observe the energetic tempo, representing the steps of the jaunty young sailor.
- Notice the contrast between the crisp, detached **staccato** and smoother, **legato** styles.
- Listen for the interpolation of 6/8 and 2/4 rhythms in the third section.
- Mark the D.C. and coda for sight-reading the piece.

 Folk Song Sheet Music: The nine folk songs heard in *English Folk Song Suite* are provided in sheet music form with melody and multiple verses. They may be printed for study or performance from the CD-rom.

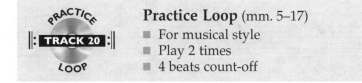

Practice Loop (mm. 5–17)
- For musical style
- Play 2 times
- 4 beats count-off

MM. 5–17 Folk Melody Study

Seventeen Come Sunday

As I rose up one May morning
One May morning so early
I overtook a pretty fair maid,
Just as the sun was dawnin' with me
Rue rum ray, fother diddle ay,
Wok fol air diddle ido.

Focus:

- Observe *pp* dynamic level.
- Play the melody softly enough, as if you are whispering the tune.
- 8th notes should be light, compact and detached.
- Contrast the 1st four measures with the more smooth, lyric style in mm. 8–11.

MM. 1–4 Music Excerpt (Study in dynamic control)

Focus:

- Begin with a full, confident *f*, then diminuendo over eight beats to *p*.
- Each beat must become gradually, but appreciably softer (*f*, *mf*, *mp*, *p*).
- Melodic style: short, short, stretch.
- Listen for the statement and answer between high and low voices.
- Practice at a slower tempo for better control.
- This introduction functions to set up the *pp* level of the first statement of the melody.

MM. 33–40 Music Excerpt (Balance and finesse on release)

Pretty Caroline

One morning in the month of May,
How lovely shone the sun,
All on the banks of the daisies gay
There sat a lonely one.
She did appear as goddess fair
And her dark brown hair did shine.
It shaded her neck and bosom fair
Of my pretty Caroline.

Focus:

- The melody should be expressively shaped, with a lyrical, singing tone quality.
- **Accompaniment** lines should balance (and be softer than) the melody.
- All 8th notes followed by a rest should not be short; rather, slightly stretched and taper into silence for proper finesse on releases.
- Slurred bass lines should sound smooth and effortless.

Rhythm Exercise

Focus:

- Practice each line separately on assigned pitches.
- **A Line:**
  - 6/8 rhythm: play the dotted eighths long, with slight stress.
  - All 8th notes are short, crisp, and secco (dry).
  - Fast air and quick "pulling back" of tip of tongue will facilitate articulation.
- **B Line:**
  - Players must mentally subdivide duple time to avoid lapsing into 6/8 rhythms.
  - Think ♫♫ on all ♫.
  - **Marcato** style requires slightly longer, but still detached 8th notes.
  - Quarter notes are accented.

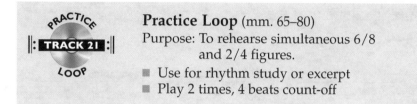

Practice Loop (mm. 65–80)
Purpose: To rehearse simultaneous 6/8 and 2/4 figures.
- Use for rhythm study or excerpt
- Play 2 times, 4 beats count-off

MM. 65–80 Music Excerpt (6/8 vs. 2/4)

Dives and Lazarus

As it fell out upon one day,
Rich Diverus he made a feast;
And he invited all his friends
And gentry of the best.
And it fell out upon one day,
Poor Lazarus he was so poor,
He came and laid him down and down,
Ev'n down at Diverus' door.

Focus:

- All players must maintain integrity of **polymetric** character.
- Good balance must be maintained between 2/4 and 6/8 melodies.
- Maintain intensity in long notes; bring out moving quarter notes.
- The 2/4 melody must create energy with the air, not with heavy tongues.

MM. 18–30 + Coda Music Excerpt

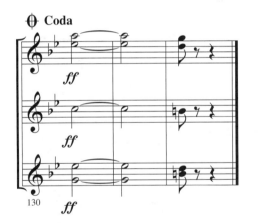

Focus:

- Melodic 8th notes should be light, compact and detached.
- Tonguing should remain light, even at *ff* dynamic level.
- At **phrase** ends, 8th notes followed by rests should be lengthened slightly.
- **Accompaniment** 8th notes should be crisply articulated and follow the melodic line phrasing.
- Bring out all quarter note accompaniment voices – mm. 20, 21, 23, 24.
- Half notes in the coda should intensify to the last note.
- Listen for the **Picardy third** (changes chord from minor to major).
- Careful balance and tuning is required of the final two chords.
- Stretch the last 8th note so that it rings into silence.

Listening Experience

Mvt. II: Intermezzo – "My Bonny Boy"

Focus:

- Observe how Vaughan Williams skillfully captures the contrasting moods of the two folksongs.
- Notice how soft, **legato** attacks and beautifully shaped **phrase** lines enhance the piece.
- Listen for the excellent and expressive tone qualities of the solo voices.

MM. 3–9 Folk Melody Study

My Bonny Boy

I once loved a boy, a bonny, bonny boy,
I loved him, I'll vow and protest;
I loved him so well and so very, very well,
That I built him a berth on my breast.

Focus:

- This beautiful melody must be played with a soft but intense tone quality.
- All attacks are smooth and **legato**—use "doo" or "du" syllable.
- Melodic line should be expressively **phrased**.
- Dotted line crescendos are only suggestions for phrasing.
- Take care not to accent the upper note of the **octave** slur. In fact, the octave slur may be more musical if the upper note is softer than the lower tone.
- Stretch the release on beat 2 of m. 6, followed by a quick breath and gentle re-entry on the pickups to m. 7.

MM. 1–10 + Final Chord Music Excerpt (Controlled attacks/releases/balance/tuning)

* release into silence

Focus:

- Initiation of tone on pp chords should be executed with a soft, gentle legato articulation.
- Notes followed by rests should taper into the solo entrance so that no space occurs between the end of one voice and the beginning of another.
- Accompaniment voices must be played very softly and sensitively, and should not cover the melodic line.
- Chordal balance and tuning is pivotal to the success of this movement.
- The final chord should be carefully balanced and tuned.
- Cresc. and decresc. on the last chord is subtle and should not exceed mp level.
- Watch your director for a tapered release of the last 8th note.

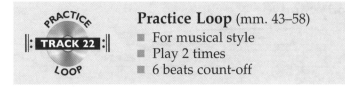

Practice Loop (mm. 43–58)
- For musical style
- Play 2 times
- 6 beats count-off

MM. 43–58 (Folk melody – scherzando style)

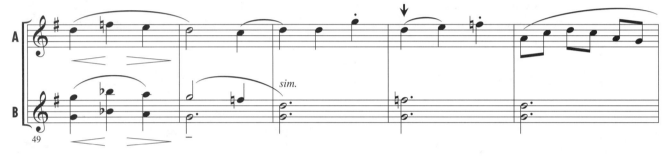

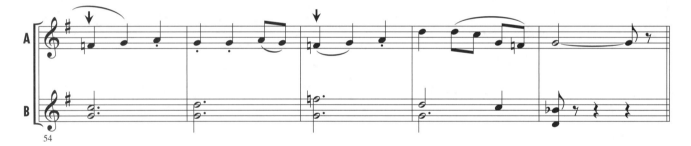

Green Bushes

As I was a-walking one morning in Spring,
For to hear the birds whistle and the nightingales sing,
I saw a young damsel, so sweetly sang she:
Down by the green bushes he thinks to meet me.

Focus:

- This **staccato** articulation should be light and detached to capture the playful nature of this section. The first beat of each measure should be stressed slightly (↓ = stress).
- The dynamic level remains soft and delicate.
- The quick crescendo/decrescendo should be emphasized, but not exaggerated.
- Part B represents a bagpipe accompaniment (**drone**) – listen carefully to tune the open intervals.
- For added effect, add a slight accent on the **drone** downbeat, followed by a diminuendo.

Listening Experience TRACK 6

Mvt. III: March – "Folk Songs from Somerset"

Focus:

- ■ Listen for contrasting dynamics, light style, and brisk tempo.
- ■ Notice how Vaughan Williams contrasts the lyricism of the solo voice with a light **staccato** second phrase.
- ■ When each folksong begins, hear how the style captures the energy of the text.
- ■ Observe how Vaughan Williams uses low brass and woodwinds to portray the powerful masculine style of the war-like "High Germany," and "John Barleycorn" at mm. 29 and 89.
- ■ Hear the lilting and contrasting style of the 6/8 "Whistle, Daughter, Whistle" theme.

Vaughan Williams closes the *Folk Song Suite* with a rousing and energetic march in which he uses the folksongs, "Blow Away the Morning Dew," "High Germany," "Whistle, Daughter, Whistle," and "John Barleycorn." Vaughan Williams enjoyed collecting folksongs in the Somerset region of England, and he found this area to be exceedingly picturesque. Crossed with many hills offering magnificent views of the English countryside, the County of Somerset includes castles and abbeys, great houses and gardens as well as picturesque thatched cottages and rural farmland. All four folk tunes are adapted well into Vaughan Williams' march setting, with each contributing contrasting material and providing a fitting conclusion to the *English Folk Song Suite*.

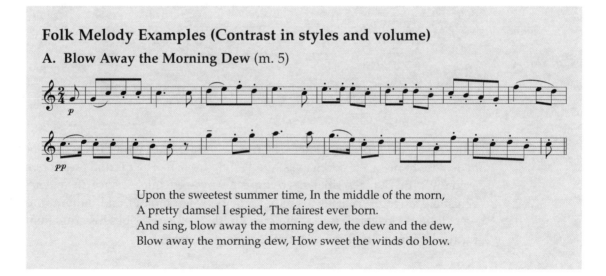

Folk Melody Examples (Contrast in styles and volume)

A. Blow Away the Morning Dew (m. 5)

Upon the sweetest summer time, In the middle of the morn,
A pretty damsel I espied, The fairest ever born.
And sing, blow away the morning dew, the dew and the dew,
Blow away the morning dew, How sweet the winds do blow.

Often folksingers used the same melody to tell a different story. Below is another version of "Blow Away the Morning Dew:"

There was a farmer's son
Kept sheep all on the hill;
And he walked out one May morning to see what he could kill.
And sing...etc.

B. High Germany (m. 29)

O Polly, O Polly, the rout has now begun,
And we must march away at the beating of the drum.
Go dress yourself all in your best, and come along with me,
I'll take you to the cruel wars in High Germany.

C. Whistle, Daughter, Whistle (m. 73)

Mother I long to get married, I long to be a bride;
I long to be with that young man, forever by his side;
Forever by his side, Oh, how happy I should be…

D. John Barleycorn (m. 89)

There was three men come from the West. Their frolics for to try.
They vowed and swear and did declare John Barleycorn should die.

"Blow Away the Morning Dew" describes a young man who flirts with a beautiful damsel. She is wise to his ways and leaves him feeling foolish. The martial and robust style of "High Germany" (m. 39) describes a young man pressed into service in a war with Germany. "Whistle, Daughter, Whistle" is a dialogue between mother and daughter. History does not reveal John Barleycorn's transgressions, but this song describes his cruel demise at the hands of three Irishmen. (Refer to CD-rom for complete texts.)

Focus:
- Observe the varied styles and dynamics:
  a. *p* dynamic level, light, compact **staccato**
  b. *ff* dynamic level, **marcato** style, stress on dotted quarter notes
  c. *p* dynamic level, lilting 6/8 meter, light
     staccato, but not as short as "a"
  d. *ff* dynamic level, accented quarter notes, detached 8th notes
- *p* dynamics must be played softly, but still projected with fast air and good **resonance**.
- *ff* dynamics must be full and confident, taking care to avoid heavy, bombastic tonguing.
- The march style requires detached 8th notes unless otherwise notated.

MM. 61–68 Music Excerpt (March style)

Focus:

- **Unison** and **octave** melody parts should "listen down" to lower parts for better intonation.
- Harmony voices should blend with the melody, but not cover it.
- An extremely fast, energized air stream is necessary to produce the required *ff* dynamic.
- **Staccato** 8th notes should be played in a crisp, compact manner.
- "Listen vertically" for good rhythmic alignment; all notes should be the same length.
- Longer note values (♪. ♩ ♩.) should be emphasized with added weight or stress.
- The last note in m. 68 should be longer and stronger than preceding 8th notes, and must create a feeling of finality on the Bb chord.

Special Techniques...

"Listen down" – listen for the lowest notes in the ensemble sonority as a reference for pitch and balance. (Ex. – flutes and trumpets listen to the low brass to adjust their pitch and balance)

"Listen vertically" – for precision, listen carefully to the entire ensemble to synchronize placement and lengths of individual notes, rhythmic figures and other elements.

MM. 71–88 Music Excerpt – Trio (Contrasts in 6/8 time)

Focus:

- The tempo remains the same throughout the 6/8 section.
- Introductory 8th notes must decrescendo from *ff* to *pp* in a rapid 4 counts.
- The woodwind melody should listen critically and match pitch.
- Include slight stress or weight on long note values, "toss off"(soften) the 8th notes.
- Accompaniment 8th notes should remain light and soft, but must still resonate.
- ♪♪♪ ♪ figure (m. 76 & 80) is important. Play the first 8th slightly longer with more volume, then rapidly decrescendo.

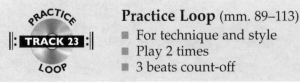

Practice Loop (mm. 89–113)
- For technique and style
- Play 2 times
- 3 beats count-off

MM. 89–113 Music Excerpt (Balancing melody and fanfare)

Focus:

- Two important musical ideas occur simultaneously and should be equally balanced:
    - A. Melody: "John Barleycorn" (low brass, sxs, low ww)
    - B. Fanfare-like passage: (hns, tpts, ww)
- The melody should be played with aggressive, centered fortissimo tone quality.
- A release on beat 1 of the melodic line (m. 96), followed by a full breath, will enhance the martial style.
- Fanfare-like passages should be crisply articulated and rhythmically precise.
- Adding a slight decrescendo in m. 102 will enhance the crescendo m. 103.
- The accents starting at m. 105 require energy on the initiation of tone and a rapid decay of sound to capture the high point of this movement.
- The 2nd note in last measure must be full and resonant.

Creative Activities

- Sing one or more of the folk songs found in *English Folk Song Suite*. Lyrics are provided on the CD-rom.
- Discuss how technology changed the ways people experience music.
- Reflect on an historical event that has made an impact on your life. Invite a friend to listen to you improvise, on your instrument, a melody that reflects your thoughts about that event and get their reaction.

Composer Profile

Percy Aldridge Grainger
(1882–1961)

Percy Aldridge Grainger, revered as a musical genius, was born in Melbourne, Australia on July 8, 1882. His writing for band represents one of the most innovative and creative minds of the 20th century. During his lifetime, Grainger achieved great fame as a concert pianist. He was handsome and talented, and treated by his audiences much like a rock star would be treated today.

Upon his refusal to return to school after witnessing the torment of a helpless animal by his classmates, Grainger was home-schooled by his mother, Rose. Grainger's father, John, an architect and engineer, suffered from alcoholism, and provided little influence on his son's life. When Percy was 5 years old, Rose gave him piano lessons, and insisted that he practice two hours every day. Rose was a stern teacher, who rewarded her talented young son when he showed exemplary progress, and punished him when he failed to meet her exacting standards. Percy never seemed to mind his mother's sternness. He remained a close and devoted son until her death.

A precocious child, Grainger began writing letters that demonstrated an extraordinary vocabulary for a boy of five. He also developed a fascination for Anglo-Saxon and Old Norse literature, reading such epics as *Beowulf*, when most children his age were still reading nursery rhymes. At age 10, Grainger began studying piano with Lewis Pabst, and at age 12, he performed his first recital. When Grainger was 13, his mother took him to Frankfurt-am-Main, Germany, where he studied at the Hoch Conservatory.

In May 1901, Grainger and his mother sailed to England, where the talented young musician soon established himself as a serious and much sought after concert pianist. It was during his time in England that Grainger became an admirer and collector of folk songs. Equipped with a heavy Edison-Bell cylinder phonograph, he became the first folksong collector in England to make live recordings of the singers. Grainger's determination to capture the spirit and individuality of each singer led to his unique ability to notate extremely complex rhythms with astounding accuracy.

In 1915, Grainger and his mother moved to the United States, where he ultimately became an American citizen. During World War I, Grainger enlisted in an army band, where he strengthened his knowledge of brass, woodwind and percussion instruments. He developed a fondness for the saxophone and double reed instruments that were to become prominently featured in his numerous wind compositions. Rich, vibrant harmonic language, as well as complicated, asymmetrical meters also characterize Grainger's works for band.

Grainger led an unusual, eclectic lifestyle. An avid physical fitness buff, he would often walk or run the 40–50 mile distance between cities rather than use conventional transportation. He was a vegetarian, and refused to drink alcohol. Once, while on a ship, Grainger was discovered shoveling coal in the boiler room to keep in shape during the voyage.

While composing music, he steadfastly refused to use the customary Italian terms in his music, preferring to incorporate phrases such as "louden lots," "hammeringly," and "jogtrottingly." Inspired by sheer genius, Grainger attempted to construct, in his own words, a "free music machine." This machine would produce gliding tones and complex rhythms, and would eliminate the "tyranny of the performer" by transferring music directly from the composer to the listener. This innovative concept of a music machine, of course, represented the first efforts toward the invention of the modern synthesizer, and serves to illustrate that Grainger was a man well ahead of his time.

During his lifetime, Grainger wrote or arranged over 1,200 musical compositions. Among his most well-known works for band are: *Australian Up-Country Tune, Children's March, Colonial Song, Down Longford Way, Handel In The Strand, Irish Tune from County Derry, Lincolnshire Posy, Molly on the Shore, Shepherd's Hey,* and the *Sussex Mummers' Christmas Carol.* His compositions continue to be widely celebrated, and the concert band world remains forever in his debt.

Ye Banks and Braes O'Bonnie Doon

Percy Aldridge Grainger

Introduction to the Music

Ye Banks and Braes O'Bonnie Doon is based on an old Scottish melody, possibly a Scottish piping tune. The Doon is a river in Alloway, Scotland. A "brae" is a hillside along a river. In the key of F major, *Ye Banks and Braes O'Bonnie Doon* is only 33 measures in length and the melody contains only five notes: f-g-a-c-d. These five notes form a **pentatonic scale**.

The folksong is based upon a poem, "The Banks 'O Doon," by the famous Scottish poet, Robert Burns. The poem describes a tragic love affair.

Ye banks and braes O'bonnie Doon
How can ye bloom so fresh and fair?
How can ye chant, ye little birds,
While I'm so weary, full o' care?
Thou'lt break my heart, thou warbling bird,
That filters thru the flowering thorn,
Thou reminds me of departed joys,
Departed - never to return.

You'll break my heart, thou bonny bird,
That sings beside thy mate,
For so I sat, and so I sang.
But knew not of my fate.
Oft did we roam by bonny Doon,
To see the rose and woodbine twine,
Where every bird sang of its love,
And fondly so did I for mine.

With lightsome heart, I pulled a rose
So sweet upon its thorny tree,
But my false lover stole my rose,
And ah! He left the thorn with me.
With lightsome heart I pulled a rose,
Upon a morn in June,
And so I flowered in the morn,
And so was ruined by noon.

More about...

Robert Burns (1759–1796). Famous Scottish poet whose use of the Scottish dialect in his verses brought an element of freshness into English poetry. His most famous verses include "Auld Lang Syne," and "Comin' thru the Rye." A longer Burns poem, "Tam 'O Shanter" was set to music by the English composer, Malcolm Arnold.

Listening Experience

Focus:

- Notice how each part fits into the overall fabric of the piece.
- Observe the gentle meandering of the melody (flows like a stream).

Legato Exercise

(Concert F Major)

etc.

Boldface vocabulary words, see pages 87–88

MM. 1–8 Folk Melody Study

Focus:

- Hum or sing the melody, then imitate its expressive style on your instrument.
- Each 4-bar **phrase** should be played in one breath.
- Style should be smooth, flowing and **legato**.
- Articulation should be gentle and non-accented (whisper "doo" syllable).

MM. 10–14 Music Excerpt (Balancing voice parts)

Focus:

- Intensify on repeated note patterns or melodic ideas.
- Watch your conductor for the slowing of pulse at m. 12.

MM. 18–21 Music Excerpt (Balancing an obligato line)

Focus:

- Obligato line (picc, fl, ob, cl 1, cnt 1) should be heard, but quietly so.
- Obligato line should intensify over the barline.
- The melody (cnt 2, as 1) must be clearly heard.
- All other parts assume an accompaniment (softer) role.

MM. 26–33 Music Excerpt

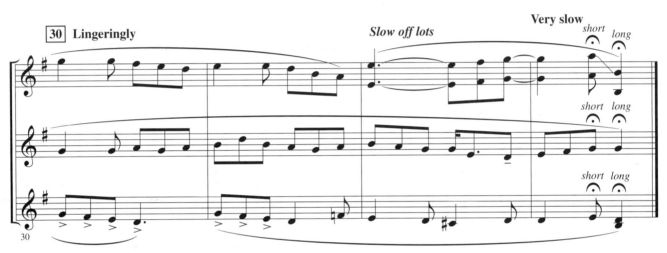

Focus:

- Intensity and expressive phrase shape are critical to this passage.
- Carefully control dynamics so that you begin *p* at m. 26 and intensify to m. 30.
- Memorize m. 26 to the end so that you may better follow your director.

Creative Activities

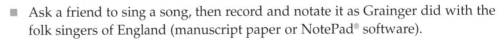

- Ask a friend to sing a song, then record and notate it as Grainger did with the folk singers of England (manuscript paper or NotePad® software).
- Select another composition currently being studied and rewrite all the terms for dynamics, articulation and tempo in a Grainger style.
- Log on to *www.halleonard.com/EMband* for links to websites about Percy Aldridge Grainger.

Historical Timelines

English Composers

American Composers

English Composers

1870	1880	1890	1900	1910

• Ralph Vaughan Williams born (October 12, 1872)

• RVW enters Royal College of Music and meets close friend Holst (1891)

RVW becomes member of Folk Song Society (1904) •

RVW premiers *Fantasia on a Theme of Tallis* (1910) •

RVW begins teaching at the Royal College of Music (1919) •

Vaughan Williams

• Gustavus Theodore von Holst born – changes name to Gustav Holst at the outbreak of WWI (September 21, 1874)

• Holst enters Royal College of Music (1893)

Holst succeeds RVW as music director at St. Paul's Girls' School (1905) •

Holst composes *First Suite in E♭* (1909) •

Holst composes *Second Suite in F* (1911) •

Holst

• Percy Aldridge Grainger born (July 8, 1882)

Grainger arrives in England to be a concert pianist (1901) •

Grainger meets Grieg (1906) •

Grainger becomes an American citizen (1919) •

Grainger

• John D. Rockefeller founds Standard Oil Company (1870)

• Mark Twain writes *Adventures of Tom Sawyer* (1875)

• Alexander Graham Bell invents telephone (1876)

• Thomas Edison invents the phonograph, lightbulb and movie projector (1877–1888)

• Paris hosts the World's Fair (1878)

• Rodin sculpts *The Thinker* (1880)

• Oxford English dictionary begins publication (1884)

• Rimsky-Korsakov composes *Sheherazade* (1888)

• Tchaikovsky's *The Nutcracker* premieres (1892)

• First modern Olympics take place in Athens, Greece (1896)

• The Spanish-American War (1898)

First Tour de France (1903) •

London Symphony gives its first concert (1904) •

Mahler completes *Symphony No. 8* (1907) •

Roald Amundsen reaches the South Pole (1911) •

Calypso music is first recorded in Trinidad (1914) •

Bolsheviks execute Czar Nicholas II and family (1918) •

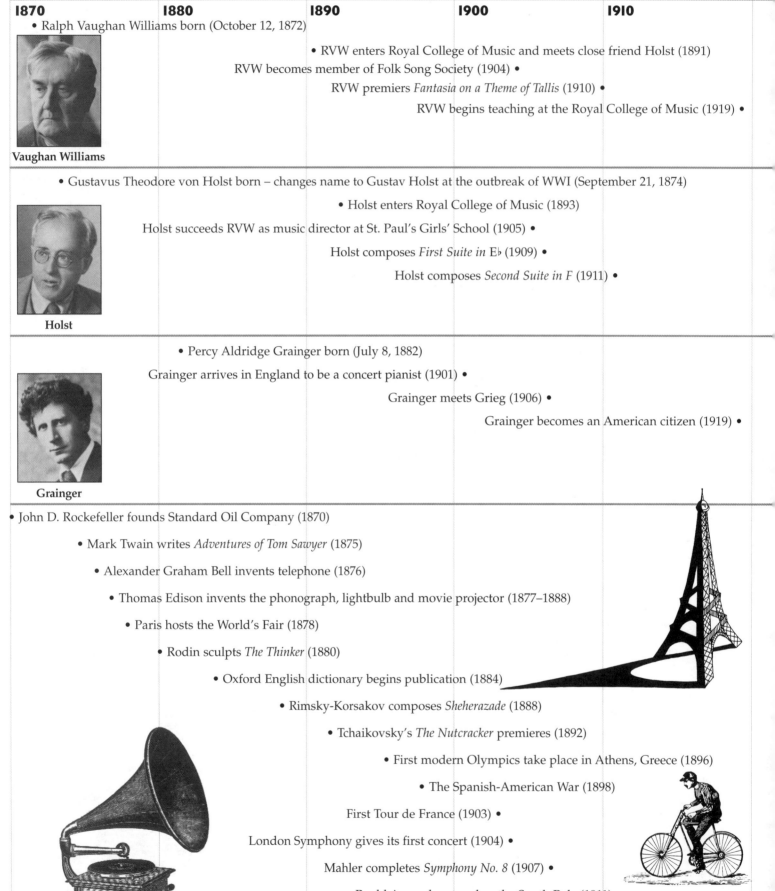

1920	1930	1940	1950	1960

• RVW composes *Rhosymedre* (1920)

  • RVW premiers *English Folk Song Suite* (1923)

        • RVW becomes President of The English Folk Dance and Song Society (1932)

              • RVW writes first film score "49th Parallel" (1940)

                    RVW dies (August 26,1958) •

• *The Planets* first complete performance in London (1920)

          • Holst dies (May 25, 1934)

        • Grainger scores *Ye Banks and Braes O'Bonnie Doon* for band (1932)

              • Grainger composes *Lincolnshire Posy* (1937)

                    Grainger dies (February 20, 1961) •

  • *Time* magazine founded (1923)

    • Hitler publishes *Mein Kampf, Vol. 1* (1925)

      • Philo Farnsworth patents first television (1927)

      • Babe Ruth hits 60 home runs for the New York Yankees (1927)

        • Amelia Earhart is first woman to fly across the Atlantic (1928)

        • Completion of the Empire State Building (1931)

          • Jesse Owens wins four gold medals at the Olympics in Berlin (1936)

            • World War II begins (1939)

            • Philip Levine and Rufus Stetson discover Rh factor in human blood (1939)

              • Aaron Copland composes *A Lincoln Portrait* (1943)

                • Invasion of Normandy by Allied forces (1944)

                  • First atomic bombs dropped on Hiroshima and Nagasaki (1945)

                • Discovery of the Dead Sea Scrolls (1947)

      J.R.R. Tolkien publishes *The Lord of the Rings* (1954) •

      Transatlantic cable telephone service (1956) •

        My Fair Lady opens on Broadway (1958) •

          Construction of the Berlin Wall (1961) •

American Composers

1880	1890	1900	1910	1920	1930

• Robert Russell Bennett born (June 15, 1894)

• Bennett's first conducting experience at age 11 (1905)

• Bennett goes to New York (1916)

Bennett

• Leonard Bernstein born (August 25, 1918)

Bernstein graduates Harvard University (June 22, 1939) •

Bernstein

John Barnes Chance born (November 20, 1932) •

Chance

• Assassination of US President Garfield (1881)

• Tchaikovsky *1812 Overture* premieres (1882)

• Mark Twain writes *Huckleberry Finn* (1884)

• Statue of Liberty dedication (1886)

• N. Dakota, S. Dakota, Montana, and Washington become states (1889)

• Establishment of Nobel Prizes for physics, physiology and medicine, chemistry, literature and peace (1896)

• First magnetic recording of sound (1898)

• Aaron Copland born (1900)

• Orville and Wilbur Wright fly a powered airplane (1903)

• Ford Motor Company produces the first Model T (1908)

• Titanic sinks (1912)

Jeannette Rankin becomes the first woman elected to Congress (1916) •

19th Amendment gives women the right to vote (1920) •

George Gershwin's *Rhapsody in Blue* premieres (1923) •

First talking movie *The Jazz Singer* premieres (1927) •

Clyde Tombaugh discovers the planet Pluto (1930) •

Franklin D. Roosevelt wins Presidential election (1932) •

Completion of Hoover Dam creating Lake Meade (1936) •

1940	1950	1960	1970	1980	1990

• Bennett composes *Suite of Old American Dances* (1949)

• Bennett wins an Oscar for the music of *Oklahoma!* (1955)

• Bennett composes *Symphonic Songs for Band* (1957)

• Bennett dies (August 18, 1981)

• Bernstein premieres *Jeremiah* conducting the Pittsburgh Symphony Orchestra (1944)

• Bernstein conducts *Overture to Candide* (January 26, 1957)

• *West Side Story* wins ten Oscars (1961)

• Bernstein appointed music director of New York Philharmonic (1958-1969)

Bernstein receives the Kennedy Center Honors (1980) •

Bernstein dies (October 14, 1990) •

• Chance joins the US Army and is sent to Seoul, Korea (1957)

• Chance composes *Incantation and Dance* (1960)

• Chance composes *Variations on a Korean Folk Song* (1965)

• Chance wins Ostwald Award for *Variations on a Korean Folk Song* (1966)

• Chance dies (August 16, 1972)

• Discovery of The Lascaux Caves in France with prehistoric wall paintings approximately 20,000 years old (1940)

• Aaron Copland writes *Rodeo* (1942)

• Victory in Europe (VE) Day (1945)

• CBS presents the first color television broadcast in the US (1951)

• Hillary and Norgay reach the summit of Mt. Everest (1953)

• Oral polio vaccine developed by Albert Sabin (1956)

• First satellite, *Sputnick I,* launched into space by Soviet Union (1957)

• Alaska becomes 49th state (1958)

• Fidel Castro becomes Premier of Cuba (1959)

• Pop Art show at New York Guggenheim Museum (1963)

• Assassination of U.S. President John F. Kennedy (November 22, 1963)

• First manned lunar landing by the United States (1969)

• Kennedy Center for the Performing Arts opens (1971)

• United States celebrates its Bicentennial (1976)

IBM launches the home or personal computer (1981) •

Space Shuttle *Challenger* explodes after lift-off (1986) •

George Bush wins Presidential election (1988) •

Englishman Timothy Berner-Lee introduces the World Wide Web, allowing universal access to the Internet (1989) •

Exxon *Valdez* causes the world's largest oil spill in Alaska (1989) •

Composer Profile

Robert Russell Bennett
(1894–1981)

Photo courtesy of Cleveland Library

Robert Russell Bennett is heralded as "the Dean of American arrangers." Bennett was born in Kansas City, Missouri, on June 15, 1894, and throughout his lifetime, he became equally renowned as a composer and conductor. His father, a band-master, and his mother, who taught him to play the piano, guided Bennett's early musical development. Although he started performing as a brass player, Bennett was often asked to substitute for whatever instrument was missing from his father's band. He was known as the band's utility member who could "borrow a horn and play whatever was missing at rehearsals, parades and celebrations."[1] Bennett was also an organist in a Kansas City theater, and played violin and viola in local string ensembles. He made his first appearance as a conductor at age 11. It was evident that the musical seeds planted in Bennett's early life would help him mature into one of the world's most skillful orchestrators.

Bennett studied harmony and composition with Carl Busch, the Danish composer, who was the founder and first conductor of the Kansas City Symphony Orchestra. Busch was generous in his praise of Bennett, and credited him with being able to "solve the most difficult problems in counterpoint with the greatest ease."[2] Along with his fellow students, Aaron Copland and Roger Sessions, Bennett also studied composition with Nadia Boulanger in Paris, who regaled him as "a true artist."[3]

In 1916, Bennett moved to New York to pursue his musical career. He started as a copyist for G. Schirmer and T. B. Harms, and eventually accepted a promotion as an arranger. By the 1950s, Bennett had earned the reputation of "the Dean of American arrangers." A man of great modesty, he was said to remark, "The way you become the dean of anything is simply to live longer than everyone else in your field."[4] Bennett is credited with orchestrating all or part of over 300 Broadway shows while collaborating with the great Broadway composers, Irving Berlin, George Gershwin, Jerome Kern, Cole Porter and Richard Rodgers. In addition to numerous other awards, medals, and citations, Bennett received an Academy Award for his orchestration of the film score *Oklahoma!* He also arranged and conducted the music composed by Richard Rodgers for the World War II Pacific theater documentary *Victory at Sea.*

Despite the exhausting task of orchestrating up to 20 Broadway shows per season, Bennett remained active as a composer of orchestral music, chamber music, keyboard and vocal works, and film scores. His compositions for concert band number over two dozen, and include *Suite of Old American Dances* (1949) and *Symphonic Songs for Band* (1957). These two compositions, scored with the masterful simplicity and clarity that have become Bennett's trademark, are still considered to be classics of the concert band repertoire.

Culver Pictures

With Frederick Fennell

Louis Ouzer Archive,
Sibley Music Library,
Eastman School of Music

[1] Ferencz, George J., *The Broadway Sound: The Autobiography and Selected Essays of Robert Russell Bennett*, p. 24.

[2] *Ibid.*, p. 34.

[3] *Ibid.*, p. 96.

[4] *Ibid.*, p. 2.

Suite of Old American Dances

Robert Russell Bennett

Introduction to the Music

Robert Russell Bennett and his wife Louise attended a Carnegie Hall concert on January 3, 1948 featuring the renowned Goldman Band with Goldman conducting. This was a special event sponsored by the League of Composers in honor of Goldman's 70th birthday. Bennett reflected on his reaction to the special concert by remarking:

Electric Park, Kansas City; ca. 1900

I suddenly thought of all the beautiful sounds the American concert band could make that it hadn't yet made. That doesn't mean that the unmade sounds passed in review in my mind at all, but the sounds they made were so new to me after all my years with orchestra, dance bands, and tiny "combos" that my pen was practically jumping out of my pocket begging me to give this great big instrument some more music to play.[1]

To set his inspiration to music, Bennett was moved to write his original wind band composition, *Suite of Old American Dances,* and he is quoted as saying, "To satisfy all this urging I found time to put a good-sized piece on paper. There was no such thing as spare time for me at that time, but somehow I got a part done here and a part done there and one day there was a piece to show Dr. Edwin Franko Goldman to see if he was interested in adding one more idiom to his collection."[2] Bennett completed the condensed score in 1948 and wrote out the individual parts over a period of a year and a half, as he simultaneously orchestrated Cole Porter's *Kiss Me Kate,* Richard Rodgers' *South Pacific,* and numerous other assignments that included shows, music for radio and television, and a few compositions of smaller scope.

Bennett originally titled his work *Electric Park* to pay tribute to the park in Kansas City that had so impressed him in his childhood. He writes, "The tricks with big electric signs, the illuminated fountains, the big band concerts, the scenic railway and the big dance hall – all magic. In the dance hall all afternoon and evening you could hear the pieces the crowd danced to."[3] The title *Electric Park* was never used, as the composition was titled *Suite of*

Old American Dances at the time of publication. Bennett commented at that time, "I had a nice name for it, but you know how publishers are – they know their customers, and we authors never seem to."[4] The piece was divided into five movements that reflected popular dances of the day.

Electric Park at night; Kansas City; ca. 1910

[1] Ferencz, George J., *The Broadway Sound: The Autobiography and Selected Essays of Robert Russell Bennett.* pp. xi–xii.   [2] *Ibid.,* p. 200.   [3] *Ibid.,* pp. 200–201.   [4] *Ibid.,* p. 200.

Listening Experience

Mvt. I: "Cake Walk"

The **cakewalk** dance is generally associated with **ragtime** music and its many syncopated rhythms. The dance had a Black American origin that was parodied in minstrel shows, vaudeville, and burlesque. Early origins indicate that dancers, dressed in fancy clothing to mimic the plantation owners, would prance and strut arm and arm, bowing and kicking backwards and forwards, as they saluted the spectators in a grand march fashion. The outstanding dancers were awarded the prize of a cake that was then shared with the other contestants.

Focus:

- Listen to the basic style before sight-reading the music.
- The rhythmic interpretation is critical to the style.
- In Ragtime/Jazz, short notes are played longer, and long notes are played shorter.
- The style concept must be understood before the music can "escape" the printed page.

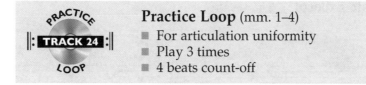

Practice Loop (mm. 1–4)
- For articulation uniformity
- Play 3 times
- 4 beats count-off

MM. 1–4 Cake Walk

Focus:

- "Dut" indicates a short note, not stopping the tone with the tongue.
- Give added weight to offbeat **syncopations**.
- Upper instruments should "listen down" through the band; **octave** tunings are critical.

Special Technique...

"**Listen down**" – listen for the lowest notes in the ensemble sonority as a reference for pitch and balance. (Ex. – flutes and trumpets listen to the low brass to adjust their pitch and balance)

Boldface vocabulary words, see pages 87–88

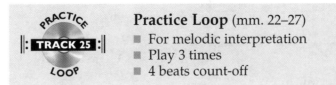

Practice Loop (mm. 22–27)
- For melodic interpretation
- Play 3 times
- 4 beats count-off

MM. 22–27 Melody Shape

Focus:

- Adding subtle ⟨ ⟩ can help shape a **phrase**.
- For maximum effect, all players must perform phrase shaping together.

MM. 98–105 Music Excerpt

Focus:

- Woodwind figures are **accompaniment** to the brass and saxophone melody.
- Woodwinds should avoid a harsh, brittle sound by playing lighter, not shorter.

MM. 140–148 Melodic "Hand-off"

Focus:

- Group B must match style and energy of Group A.
- Both parts together should create the effect of one composite melodic line.
- Although marked differently here, the cakewalk rhythm should match the style of mm. 1–4, only lighter.

MM. 158–166 Music Excerpt

Focus:

- Staccato style creates lightness, clarity, and bounce.

- Avoid abrupt shortness of notes that makes the music stiff.

MM. 167–175 Music Excerpt

Focus:

- Non-melody parts should "sting and listen" to hear the melody over the harmony.

- Play the trill/tremolo as a continuous four measure event.

- "Listen down" to focus pitch and to control the "pyramid of sound" balance.

Special Technique...

"Sting and listen" – for sustained accompaniment parts that may cover other important parts. Play the appropriate dynamic and articulation, but quickly decrescendo, allowing the melodic or rhythmic part to be heard.

Listening Experience TRACK 9

Mvt. II: "Schottische"

The **schottische** is a round dance that has many similarities to the polka only executed in a slower manner. The addition of waltz-like turns to the 2/4 dance music had others characterize it as "a waltz in two." The military schottische became very popular in the United States and the dance became known as a "barn dance" in Britain. Later in the 20th century as the progressive barn dance evolved, the technique of "changing partners" was incorporated. The music for this dance is generally written in 2/4 meter and can be most simply characterized as a slow polka.

Focus:

- Listen to the Ragtime/Jazz influences of the dotted eighth/sixteenth patterns.
- Compare the style of "Schottische" to "**Cake Walk**" to observe similarities and differences.

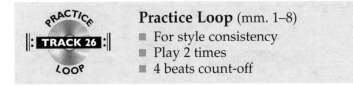

Practice Loop (mm. 1–8)
- For style consistency
- Play 2 times
- 4 beats count-off

MM. 1–8 Music Excerpt

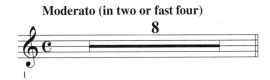

Focus:

- **Accompaniment** notes should be played in a *pizzicato* string bass style.
- Sandpaper block must be heard to create the "soft shoe" effect.

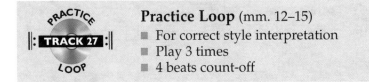

Practice Loop (mm. 12–15)
- For correct style interpretation
- Play 3 times
- 4 beats count-off

MM. 12–15 Style Etude

Focus:

- Maintain the melodic flow whether the notes are slurred (m. 12) or tongued (m. 13).
- Use a softer attack, DU-DU-DU-DU rather than TU-TU-TU-TU.

MM. 31–38 Music Excerpt

Focus:

- Strong 2nd/3rd clarinets help to stabilize the **octave** tunings.
- The melodic style should be relaxed and playful.
- Interpret dotted 8th/16th note figures as "swing 8th notes."

MM. 39–49 Music Excerpt

Focus:

- The **accompaniment** chords must be delicate to balance with the flute melody.
- Melody parts must project with ease.
- Woodwinds and trumpets should play lightly at m. 43 making sure the quarter note melody is not covered up.

Listening Experience TRACK 10

Mvt. III: "Western One-Step"

The one-step is a fast ballroom dance that became popular in both New York and England around 1910. It was danced to a fast **duple** meter march and involved the use of eight counts of walking step with a pivot on the first. Conductor Frederick Fennell shows insight into this particular one-step as he points out, "The composer informed me that this is also a dance known as the 'Texas Tommy,' an obviously bright-eyed tune with an equally bright-eyed tempo."[1] Very little has been written about the Texas Tommy other than it is a stylized dance that originated in saloons in the early 20th century. The ladies who performed this spirited dance were known as "tommies."

Focus:

- Review Balanced Chordal Structure ("The Basics of Ensemble Musicianship," p.14) to understand relative importance of upper and lower voices.
- Notice that the style and spirit rely heavily on the correct execution of the different articulations.
- The emotion and direction of the melody in this movement make for enjoyable listening.

MM. 1–10 Music Excerpt

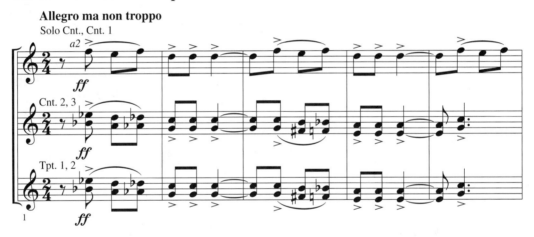

Focus:

- Maintain control and balance at extreme dynamic levels.
- Repeated patterns should show a sense of direction.
- **"Listen down"** to the low parts to tune **octaves**.
- Quicker tempo = lighter articulation.

---

[1] "Basic Band Repertory: *Suite of Old American Dances* by Robert Russell Bennett." *The Instrumentalist*, Vol. 34, No. 2, p. 35.

MM. 10–24 Music Excerpt

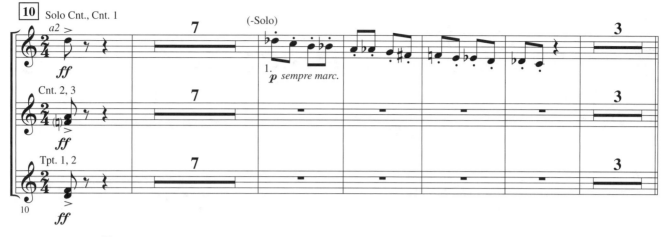

Focus:

- ◼ The clarinet melody should dominate.
- ◼ The **staccato** style is light and bouncy - avoid abrupt shortness.
- ◼ The melodic line should be supported by subtle dynamic shading.

MM. 36–47 Music Excerpt

Focus:

- ◼ Trombone/Baritone melody should project above the ensemble.
- ◼ Staccato accompaniment parts may need to be played lighter than indicated.
- ◼ A slight crescendo to the third measure of each phrase (followed by a diminuendo) gives added shape to the melody.

MM. 68–84 Music Excerpt

Focus:

- Observe the *p* dynamics to create effective contrast.
- The melody is **legato**, while the accompaniment is **staccato/marcato**.
- All players should hear the moving parts above the sustaining parts.

MM. 129–133 Two Lines Equal One

Focus:

- Be aware of the other part as well as your own.
- Balance the 2 parts to create a continuous 8th-note pattern.

MM. 179–188 Music Excerpt

Focus:

- Crescendo after the *f* only where indicated.
- Moving parts should project over the sustained *p* notes.

MM. 223–231 Music Excerpt

Focus:

- Although marked *ff*, the sustaining parts are still less important than a melodic *ff*.
- Following the initial impact and decay, the sustained notes should crescendo very slightly to support the melody.

Listening Experience   TRACK 11

Mvt. IV: "Wallflower Waltz"

The classic **waltz** that reigned as the ruler of the ballroom dance hall has survived many evolutionary changes throughout its development. The unique style of this waltz is determined much more by its title than by mere modifications to the steps. Written to add subtlety and contrast to the other faster and more energetic movements, one can immediately sense the awkward shyness of "the wallflower" as the music contrasts the stable, constant accompaniment rhythm with the tentative, lagging syncopations of the more hesitant, somewhat reluctant wallflower.

Focus:

- Note the relaxed subtlety, contrast, and **orchestration**.
- Woodwind **resonance**, control, and uniformity are critical.
- In this case, ∧ (**marcato**) must be sustained fully, unlike the more common > (accents) indication.

MM. 17–24 Music Excerpt

Focus:

- Give the accents full sustain to avoid rushing.
- **Accompaniment** pattern must be rhythmically stable and well balanced.
- The interplay between melody and accompaniment displays a playful style.

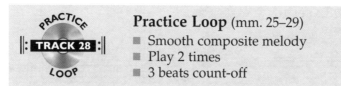

MM. 25–29 Music Excerpt

Focus:

- The rhythm lines should combine to create a smoothly connected melody.
- Maintain a playful lightness in the dotted 8th/16th note interpretation.
- Moving lines must be slightly stronger than the sustained notes.

MM. 55–62 Music Excerpt

Focus:

- Staccatos need length, weight, and "ring" to combat the tendency to push the tempo ahead.
- Maintain softness and an overall sense of relaxation.

MM. 81–96 Music Excerpt

Focus:

- ■ Balance the solo with the **countermelody**.
- ■ Moving lines need to be stronger than accompaniment figures.

Listening Experience 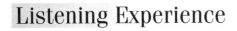 TRACK 12

Mvt. V: "Rag"

It is appropriate that Bennett chose to conclude with the style that permeates the entire suite—**ragtime**. The syncopated or ragged rhythms (thus the name "rag") along with a demand for considerable technical facility characterize this delightful suite. Addressing the subject of ragtime, Bennett once stated:

> How it got there has never been clear to me, but a piece called *The Lady with the Red Dress* was on our piano one day when I was about ten years old. I opened it and began to play it. My piano-teacher mother, who was pretty well known for brooking no nonsense, hit the ceiling. *The Lady with the Red Dress* was ragtime, and ragtime was trash. If I ever hoped to be a musician I'd better not play one more bar of it.[1]

Bennett became more than "just a musician" and the contributions of ragtime must be given their just credit for creating and energizing the unique and refreshing style of this *Suite of Old American Dances*.

[1] Ferencz, George, J., *The Broadway Sound: The Autobiography and Selected Essays of Robert Russell Bennett*, p. 9.

Focus:

- ■ The tempo is quick, but without any sense of hurrying.
- ■ Lightness is critical to **staccato** style and ensemble clarity.
- ■ Listen to the recording to review/refresh ragtime concepts.

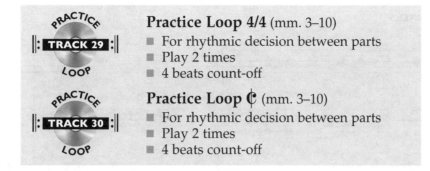

Practice Loop 4/4 (mm. 3–10)
- For rhythmic decision between parts
- Play 2 times
- 4 beats count-off

Practice Loop ¢ (mm. 3–10)
- For rhythmic decision between parts
- Play 2 times
- 4 beats count-off

MM. 3–10 Rhythm Connection

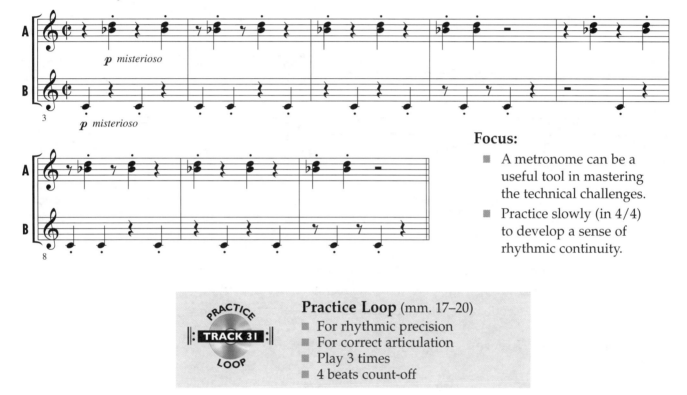

Focus:
- A metronome can be a useful tool in mastering the technical challenges.
- Practice slowly (in 4/4) to develop a sense of rhythmic continuity.

Practice Loop (mm. 17–20)
- For rhythmic precision
- For correct articulation
- Play 3 times
- 4 beats count-off

MM. 17–20 Rag Style

Focus:
- Analyze the chromatic make-up of the figure before practicing it.
- Accent the first note of each group and focus on rhythmic stability.

MM. 69–80 Music Excerpt

Focus:

- Repeated quarter notes should crescendo and move energy forward.
- Staccatos here are played in a deliberate **marcato** style.
- Crescendo on repetitive figures to create sense of direction.

MM. 113–127 Music Excerpt

Focus:

- The *p* dynamic and the **dolce** style provide dramatic contrasts to the rest of the movement.
- The **accompaniment** quarter notes should be separated but not clipped.

MM. 177–184 Music Excerpt

Focus:

- All rhythmic patterns should be precise without sounding rushed or hurried.
- Be aware of all the various elements and balance each part.

MM. 199–200 Music Excerpt

Focus:

- Drive the air stream through the repeated notes with a slight crescendo.
- Give added length and weight to the last note to express finality.

Creative Activities

- Using the Historical Timeline (pp. 44–47), select and research one historical event that occurred during Robert Russell Bennett's life. Determine if this event had any impact on music, or vice versa.
- Discuss with students what five dances should be represented if a *Suite of New American Dances* were composed.
- Listen to the music of Scott Joplin to hear other versions of "Ragtime" music.

Composer Profile

Leonard Bernstein
(1918–1990)

Leonard Bernstein, hailed as one of the most prominent American composers and conductors of the 20th century, was born in Lawrence, Massachusetts, on August 25, 1918. Bernstein is also celebrated as an accomplished pianist, author, lecturer, educator, and television personality. Although he was named Louis Bernstein by his Russian-Jewish immigrant parents, he was known as "Lenny" to family and friends. At age 16, he officially changed his name to "Leonard." As a grammar school student, Bernstein learned to sing and read music at the William L. Garrison School in Roxbury, Massachusetts. His first exposure to instrumental music occurred at age 10. As a favor to Bernstein's Aunt Clara, his family stored an upright piano that was too large for her small apartment, and young Bernstein would play it for hours at a time. His interest was rewarded and he received significant musical training from Heinrich Gebhard, who was considered to be Boston's foremost piano teacher at that time. He also benefited from the inspirational instruction of Helen Coates, who would remain by Bernstein's side throughout his life as his personal secretary.

Bernstein graduated from Boston Latin School in 1935, and entered Harvard University that same year as a music major. He became highly involved in the musical life on campus by writing reviews for the school paper, and also composed and conducted his own incidental music to Aristophanes' *The Birds*. Bernstein studied **orchestration** and harmony with noted teachers of the time, including Walter Piston, who taught him **counterpoint** and fugue. On June 22, 1939, at age 20, he graduated *cum laude*.

Beginning in 1940, Bernstein spent his summers at the Berkshire Music Center (now Tanglewood), where he studied conducting with Serge Koussevitsky, and became his assistant. He also studied composition at Tanglewood with Aaron Copland. Bernstein then entered the Curtis Institute of Music in Philadelphia, where he studied conducting with Fritz Reiner and composition with Randall Thompson.

Following a brief search for employment, Bernstein's musical career seemed to blossom all at once. His compositions (*I Hate Music*, *Jeremiah Symphony*, and the ballet *Fancy Free*) were performed to critical acclaim. He was appointed assistant conductor to Artur Rodzinski of the New York Philharmonic. Bernstein became an overnight celebrity when he directed the New York Philharmonic in a national radio broadcast by suddenly replacing the ailing Bruno Walter. He did a brilliant job of conducting the program with only a few hours' notice and little

opportunity to rehearse the orchestra. Bernstein's success on the podium earned him instant world-wide recognition as an important new conductor.

In the years that followed, Bernstein conducted numerous other major orchestras in America and Europe. In 1945, he was appointed music director of the New York Symphony Orchestra (1945-47), and in 1958, he was appointed music director of the New York Philharmonic (1958–69). More than half of Bernstein's 400+ recordings were made with the Philharmonic, where he became a champion of new American music, particularly the music of Aaron Copland.

Bernstein's accomplishments as an educator are truly remarkable. He conducted and narrated several television series with the expressed purpose of guiding viewers, both young and old, to a deeper understanding and love of high quality music. Bernstein's television appearances on *Omnibus* began in 1954, and were followed in 1958 by the first of fifty-three *Young People's Concerts*. Because of Bernstein's passionate commitment to the music education of the masses, entire generations of television viewers learned to discover, appreciate and enjoy high caliber music.

Energetic rhythms and a broad mix of traditional and jazz harmonies characterize Bernstein's compositions. His music also reflects the diversity and energy of the American spirit, as his compositions range from simple, melodic themes to ventures in twelve-tone serialism. Bernstein's works include three symphonies, three ballets, and two operas. For the theater, he composed *On the Town*, *Wonderful Town*, *Candide* and *Mass*—a piece created for singers, players, and dancers and performed in 1971 for the opening of the Kennedy Center in Washington D.C. Bernstein is perhaps best known and remembered for his highly successful Broadway musical, *West Side Story*. This modern day musical adaptation of the "Romeo and Juliet theme" enjoyed long runs on stage, and was followed by a film version that was awarded ten Oscars. Bernstein also composed numerous other works for solo instruments, orchestra, piano, and voice.

In 1990, Bernstein was ordered by his physician to retire from conducting. His death from a heart attack on October 14 of the same year brought to a close one of the most remarkable chapters of 20th-century American music. Through his influential contributions as both a musician and a teacher, Leonard Bernstein's music will continue to inspire and educate music lovers everywhere.

Overture to Candide

Leonard Bernstein

Introduction to the Music

The comic **operetta** *Candide* is based on the writings of the 18th-century French philosopher, Voltaire. Written in 1759, Voltaire's novella is a social satire that ridicules the excessive optimism set forth by Emanuel Leibniz that states we are living in the best of times, and everything that happens is for the best in the best of all possible worlds. The fact that the book was banned in Paris, publicly burned in the streets of other major cities, and placed on the Vatican Index of prohibited books practically guaranteed that the book would be a "best seller" for many editions to come.

With a book adaptation by playwright Lillian Hellman, music by Bernstein, and lyrics by Dorothy Parker, John LaTouche, Richard Wilbur and others, *Candide* opened in New York in December of 1956 after many years of preparation and revision. It closed after only 73 performances. Some critics blamed the failure on lack of story line continuity. Others found the lyrics "too literary and stubborn," while still others found fault because it lacked the characteristics of the more "traditional" Broadway musical, having no memorable tunes and no real romantic plot. Although most critics found the music to be marvelously witty and cleverly written, they questioned whether Bernstein's intention was to write an operetta or a musical. Bernstein responded to his critics by saying:

> *The particular mixture of style and elements that goes into this work makes it perhaps a new kind of show. Maybe it will turn out to be some sort of new form; I don't know. There seems to be no really specific precedent for it in our theater.*[1]

After the closing in 1957, *Candide* resurfaced in numerous guises in an effort to reach a wider, more accepting audience. First, in 1973, it was refashioned into the one-act *Chelsea*, with simplified music and enhanced staging. Then in 1982, as *City Opera*, it was elaborately designed (but without attention to the order and "message" of the music). Finally the *Scottish Opera* version of 1988 returned the operetta to Bernstein's original vision. In his book *Leonard Bernstein*, Paul Myers' evaluation of this final revision sums up the feelings of many critics who found fault with earlier versions:

> *Throughout the final version of this magnificent play-with-music/musical/**operetta**/light opera, the lyrics dazzle and delight and Bernstein's score is witty, amusing, satirical, sentimental, touching, and even deeply moving. Candide survived all its adaptations, alterations, and metamorphoses to emerge as a triumphant creation. Like any work of art, its message is universal, with continuing verities that are applicable to all times. It is a unique contribution to the musical theater of this century.*[2]

While the operetta Candide labored over a period of 30+ years to find an accepting and appreciative audience, the overture enjoyed immediate success. Bernstein led the New York Philharmonic in the first performance of the concert version of Overture to Candide on January 26, 1957. The overture opens with a typical Bernstein fanfare built on the interval of a minor seventh followed by a major second. The rest of the piece is based largely on lyrical lines from the operetta from "Oh, Happy We," and "Glitter and Be Gay" as well as musical "germs" and themes from "The Best of All Possible Worlds" and the intensely fierce "Battle Music." The overture is a masterpiece of excitement, technical challenge, and rapidly paced musical continuity. When Harold Schonberg, critic for the New York Times, first wrote in his review that this was "a smart, sophisticated little piece,"[3] little did he suspect that the Overture to Candide would become Bernstein's most popular composition in the orchestral repertoire.

[1] Ledbetter, Steven, ed. *Sennets and Tuckets: A Bernstein Celebration,* p. 44.
[2] Myers, Paul. *Leonard Bernstein,* p. 218.
[3] Burton, Humphrey. *Leonard Bernstein,* p. 266.

Boldface vocabulary words, see pages 87–88

Listening Experience

Focus:

- Listen to the variety of articulation styles including **legato**, **staccato**, and **marcato**.
- Observe the importance of technical mastery to communicate the angular lines.
- Experience the musical excitement of the light and energetic overture style.

MM. 1–6 Music Excerpt

Focus:

- Brass players must first hear the wide interval skip and use the tongue posturing AH-EE.
- The 8th notes should be double tongued.
- Staccato quarter notes should be "lifted" and may be lightly tongued.
- Woodwind trills should be played as 1-note "turns."

Practice Loop (mm. 10–19)
- For woodwind melody
- Play 2 times
- 4 beats count-off

MM. 10–19 Music Excerpt – 1st Theme

Focus:

- Upper woodwinds and 1st alto sax should practice slowly by segments (shown in excerpt) before attempting to play the entire passage.
- Low voices should accent syncopated quarter notes.
- Play the quarter note **accompaniment** figure **marcato** and defined.

MM. 32–38 Music Excerpt – 2nd Theme

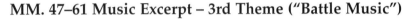

Focus:

- Melodic parts need enough length and weight to avoid rushing the tempo.
- Beat/after-beat patterns should be solid to help insure tempo stability.

MM. 47–61 Music Excerpt – 3rd Theme ("Battle Music")

Focus:

- Melody line should show distinct contrast between staccato and accented notes.
- The staccato bass line should "ring" and sound as if it were being played on timpani.
- The woodwind grace note line should "bite" with dry, marked accents.

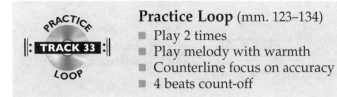

Practice Loop (mm. 123–134)
- Play 2 times
- Play melody with warmth
- Counterline focus on accuracy
- 4 beats count-off

MM. 123–134 Music Excerpt – 4th Theme ("Oh, Happy We")

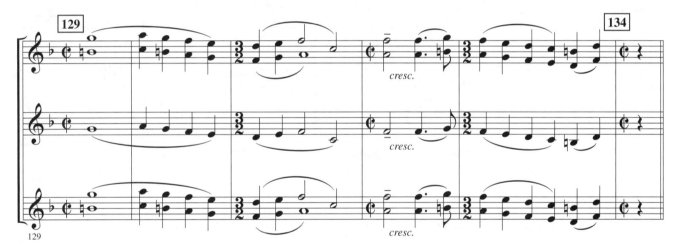

Focus:
- The melody parts must "soar" and sing with warmth and **resonance**.
- Players on the countermelody (cl. 1/2, hn., picc.) should visualize the line first, sing it next and finally play it.
- Accompaniment syncopations need enough "edge" to move the energy forward while providing a secure tempo.

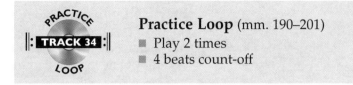

TRACK 34

Practice Loop (mm. 190–201)
- Play 2 times
- 4 beats count-off

MM. 190–201 Music Excerpt

Focus:
- Although similar to the previous excerpt, changes in **orchestration** and range create new challenges.

MM. 224–230 Music Excerpt – 5th Theme ("Glitter and Be Gay")

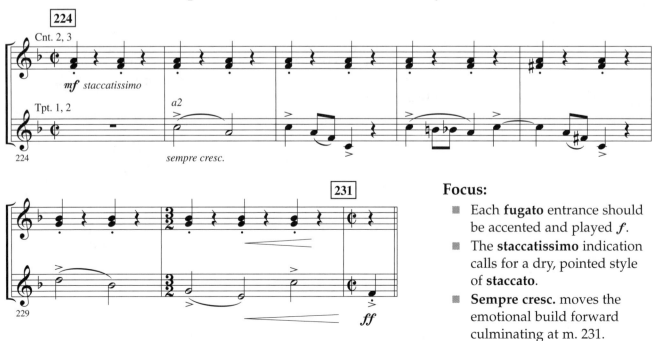

Focus:
- Each **fugato** entrance should be accented and played **f**.
- The **staccatissimo** indication calls for a dry, pointed style of **staccato**.
- **Sempre cresc.** moves the emotional build forward culminating at m. 231.

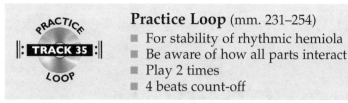

Practice Loop (mm. 231–254)
- For stability of rhythmic hemiola
- Be aware of how all parts interact
- Play 2 times
- 4 beats count-off

MM. 231–254 Music Excerpt – 6th Theme ("Glitter and Be Gay")

Focus:
- Each successive statement builds with intensity.
- Changes in articulation, however subtle, are critical to the growing musical tension.
- Become familiar with the rhythmic **accompaniment** figure to avoid possible confusion with pulse.

Creative Activities

- Using the Historical Timeline (pp. 44–47), select and research one historical event that occurred during Leonard Bernstein's life. Determine if this event had any impact on music, or vice versa.
- View the musical *West Side Story* to hear one of Bernstein's most famous musical scores.
- Read Voltaire's book *Candide*.

Composer Profile

John Barnes Chance
(1932–1972)

During his brief but brilliant career, John Barnes Chance distinguished himself as one of the most versatile and ambitious contemporary composers of multicultural repertoire for concert band. His music is hallmarked by romantic lyricism, inventive rhythmic treatments, and a creative mastery of instrumental scoring. Born in Beaumont, Texas on November 20, 1932, Chance began his formal musical training at age 9 by studying piano with Jewell Harned, a teacher he held in the highest esteem. Later, Chance remarked that he "made rapid progress as a pianist, reaching a level of proficiency by the age of 12 that he never surpassed but indeed regressed from, and now today he plays the piano in a loud and ugly manner typical of most composers."[1]

Chance played timpani in the Beaumont High School Band and Orchestra, where he developed a preference for percussion instruments with their many colorful and varied timbres. He also became fascinated with the orchestral works of Beethoven, Schubert, and Shostakovich. Chance's high school band director, Arnold Whedbee, remembers "Barney" (short for Barnes as his mother disapproved of the nickname "Jack") as "a free-spirited student, who was more interested in composing than in becoming popular with other students." Chance's serious study of composition began at age 15, and his efforts were rewarded with performances of his works while he was still in high school.

At the University of Texas-Austin, Chance studied with Clifton Williams, Kent Kennan and Paul Pisk. He received degrees in Theory and Composition (BM in 1955 and MM in 1956). During his collegiate years, Chance received the Carl Owens Award for "best student work of the year." His close association with his teacher, Clifton Williams, and his good friend, Francis McBeth, eventually led to the trio being referred to as "The Austin Three."

Following the completion of his education, Chance joined the Army in 1957 with the understanding that he would be stationed in nearby San Antonio to conduct and arrange for the Fourth Army Band. Government politics being what they are, Chance found himself assigned to the Eighth Army Band in Seoul, Korea, where he would gain the knowledge and inspiration to compose his future Ostwald Award winning composition, *Variations on a Korean Folk Song*.

Following military service, Chance returned to Texas to become timpanist with the Austin Symphony Orchestra, and also worked in the music retail business. He accepted a composer-in-residence position for the Ford Foundation Young Composers Project, and lived in Greensboro, North Carolina from 1960–1962. Chance was one of 11 composers selected from over 200 applicants. In his ambition, he is said to have composed from 6:00 p.m. until 6:00 a.m. every night. His close friend, Francis McBeth, states that Chance composed at his "disarrayed apartment, on an old upright [piano], terribly out-of-tune."

John Barnes Chance

Nevertheless, Chance's ability to charm Herbert Hazelman, Director of Bands at Greensboro High School, and his 500 young musicians kept him busy as a highly successful composer not only for band, but also for chorus, orchestra, solo instruments, and chamber ensembles.

Chance joined the music department at the University of Kentucky in 1966 as professor of Composition. He was promoted to head of theory and composition in 1971, and held that position until his untimely death. On August 16, 1972, Chance was accidentally electrocuted in his backyard when a wet canvas that he was stretching to dry came into contact with a misplaced, 200-volt electrical line.

As tribute to Chance and his music, five of his compositions were performed at the Texas Music Educators Conference in San Antonio on February 6, 1992. That performance included three published compositions and two original manuscripts provided by Herbert Hazelman. Although his tragic death at age 40 stunned the band world, John Barnes Chance's highly successful career as a gifted teacher, conductor, and composer continues to be celebrated. He wrote 20 compositions, among which the following are his most popular, published compositions: *Incantation and Dance* (1963), *Introduction and Capriccio* (1966), *Variations on a Korean Folk Song* (1967), *Blue Lake Overture* (1971), *Elegy* (1972), and *Symphony No. 2*, completed just prior to his death.

---

[1] Kopetz, Barry E., "An Analysis of Chance's *Incantation and Dance*," *The Instrumentalist*, October, 1992, p. 42.

Incantation and Dance

John Barnes Chance

Introduction to the Music

As part of the Ford Foundation Young Composers Project, John Barnes Chance spent the 1960–61 school year as composer-in-residence at the Greensboro, North Carolina public schools. His first composition for band, originally titled *Nocturne and Dance*, became *Incantation and Dance* as he deleted thirty-one bars from the original composition and changed the name to its current title. Following the premier performance on November 16, 1960, Herbert Hazelman, the high school band director, wrote, "The *Incantation and Dance* is a brilliant piece for band which has been very well received by students, townspeople, critics, musicians, and educators alike."[1] While copies of original materials for *Nocturne and Dance* still exist at Greensboro Senior High School, it is thought that Chance destroyed the original score when he revised the composition and retitled it.

An interesting performance note that Chance asked the publishers to include states his request not to play "unintended accents" in the syncopated measures in order for the mixed meter effect to come through more clearly. Chance wrote, "Because there is no musical notation to indicate a non-accent, it may be necessary to caution the players against placing any metric pulsation on the first and third beats of the syncopated measures of the dance (mm. 77, 79, 81, etc.). To accent these beats in the accustomed way will destroy the intended effect."[2]

The "**incantation**" in Chance's revised title can be defined as "words chanted in magic spells or mystical rites" and suggests the conjuring up of demons and evil spirits. As the worshipper is possessed and overwhelmed by the spirits, the result is wild and abandoned dancing that grows to a frenzied state. Chance's "Incantation" serves as the introduction to the piece and is the source of much of the melodic material that is later developed in the "Dance."

Lacking a definable **tonality**, the mood is one of wandering instability and pending anticipation as Chance explores color and **timbre** to invoke his "Incantation." The "Dance" begins quietly as well, but the continual adding of percussion instruments and rhythmic complexity causes the energy to build to a fever-like level. As the other instruments are added, the frenzy grows ever more intense as it is punctuated by driving **syncopations**, swirling woodwind passages, and intense dynamic exposures. The aural image of this mystical ritual is completed as all of these elements are skillfully combined in the coda, bringing performer and listener alike to a most satisfying and rewarding musical conclusion.

[1] Kopetz, Barry E.,"An Analysis of Chance's *Incantation and Dance*," *The Instrumentalist*, p. 42.
[2] *Ibid.*, p. 44.

Listening Experience

Focus:

- Observe the emotional effects created by tempo, dynamics, and instrumental colors.
- Identify rhythmic motives first heard in percussion and later in the winds.
- Observe the clarity of all musical elements regardless of whether the dynamic level is delicate or dramatic and intense.

Boldface vocabulary words, see pages 87–88

MM. 1–14 Music Excerpt

Focus:

- Flutes must carefully match intonation, tone color and vibrato.
- The long **phrases** are dependent on the control and volume of air intake.
- The subtle style makes uniform attacks and releases very critical.
- The clarinet **accompaniment** should be well balanced and softer than the flute melody.
- Dynamic subtleties in all parts are important to creating the mood of the "**incantation**."

MM. 27–30 Music Excerpt

Focus:

- Listen carefully to balance your part in the parallel major triads.
- If hats are not available, trumpets and trombones should play into the stands to create a diffused tone quality.
- Although marked pp and p, this section still requires good air support and resonant tone quality – soft does not mean weak!

MM. 35–54 Rhythm Study

Focus:

- Each different percussion color must contribute to clarity and balance in the proper proportion.
- Timbales should not overbalance the other delicate colors.

MM. 57–59 Unison/Octave Study

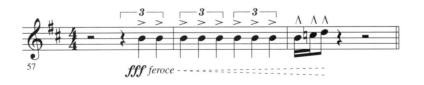

Focus:

- Start less than *fff* to leave room for a slight crescendo.
- Achieve rhythmic precision with minimal separation.
- TU-DU-DU articulation on (16th/8th note pattern) will permit greater clarity and not interrupt the air flow.

MM. 70–76 Rhythm Study

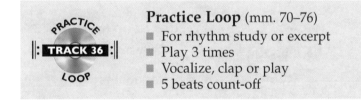

Practice Loop (mm. 70–76)
- For rhythm study or excerpt
- Play 3 times
- Vocalize, clap or play
- 5 beats count-off

MM. 70–76 Music Excerpt

Focus:

- Notice that a new 8th-note sound enters on every subdivision as the result of the A/B interplay.
- Parts must be evenly balanced and rhythmically precise to create the proper composite line.
- Work to maintain a steady tempo throughout.

MM. 101–110 Music Excerpt

Focus:

- Proper balance between moving and sustaining parts is critical to the success of this section.
- Slurred groupings should be played with attention to accents without shortening the last note in each group.
- Musical energy must flow through the rhythmic figures into the arrival notes.

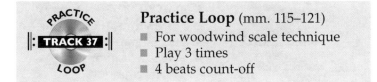

Practice Loop (mm. 115–121)
- For woodwind scale technique
- Play 3 times
- 4 beats count-off

MM. 115–121 Music Excerpt

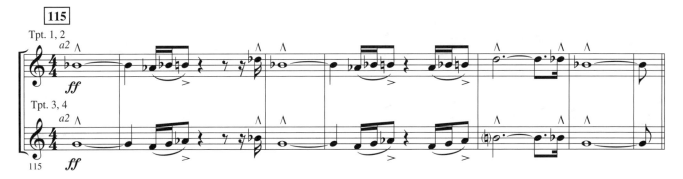

Focus:

- Scales are a combination of chromatic and whole step movement, but without recognizable pattern.
- Practice slowly to become familiar with the small grouping of patterns that do exist – mark them in pencil.
- Woodwind Scale [1] appears 3 times, Scale [2] twice and Scale [3] once.
- Playing a crescendo through each pattern will encourage air support and musical direction.

MM. 148–158 Music Excerpt

Focus:

- Balance low woodwinds/timpani with the "incantation" theme in horns and 1st clarinet.
- Avoid "blurring" the rhythmic clarity; do not hurry the 16th notes.
- Mute resistance requires horns to play f in order to obtain the effect of p.

MM. 166–175 Music Excerpt

Focus:

- Contrasts in dynamics, articulation, style, and **timbre** must be dramatic!
- Regardless of dynamic intensity, focus on good tone quality, balance, and air support.

MM. 176–187 Music Excerpt

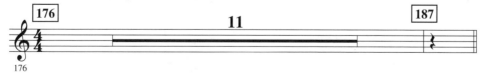

Focus:

- Flutes and clarinets should play with rhythmic accuracy so that a new color can be heard on almost every alternating 8th note.
- The contrabass clarinet should connect to the bass clarinet figure.
- The melody, first in the flutes and later in the clarinets, should dominate the highly rhythmic accompaniment.

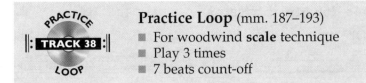

MM. 188–193 Music Excerpt

Focus:

- The combination of motives C and D (from mm. 35–54) with portions of A stated by the brass should combine to produce a continuous melodic/rhythmic composite.
- The woodwind **scales** will require slow and diligent practice.
- The implied crescendo and diminuendo in the woodwind scales adds a "swirl" of excitement to the brass melody.

MM. 207–214 Music Excerpt

Focus:

- Woodwinds should crescendo with the ascending scales and through the triplet figures.
- Brass slurs are aided with a crescendo and AH to EE tongue posturing.
- Brass – the tongue "elevates" at the last possible instant to compress and drive the air stream.

MM. 226–228 Music Excerpt

Focus:

- Start the 16th-note figure softer than *f* and play a slight crescendo.
- Note the articulation very carefully.
- Brass should match the woodwind intensity level with their entrance in m. 228.

MM. 232–235 Music Excerpt

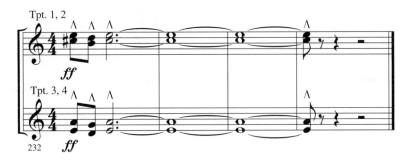

Focus:

- Rhythmic motives must combine and balance to form a single rhythmic idea.
- Sustaining parts should remain under the moving parts while supporting the forward motion with an appropriate crescendo.
- Dynamic intensity needs to develop through these measures and conclude with a "ring" that expresses full closure.

Creative Activities

- Write four 2-measure rhythms that can be played by four (or more) players to create your own drum circle (manuscript paper or NotePad®).
- Listen to a recording of Igor Stravinsky's *Rite of Spring*, a ballet composed in 1912 (50 years before *Incantation and Dance*), symbolizing ancient Slavic tribe rituals.
- Log on to *www.halleonard.com/EMband* for links to websites about the popular music of 1960, the year Chance composed *Incantation and Dance*.

Scales and Arpeggios

Major Scales

Play major scales as part of your daily practice routine. Play all octaves, keys, and arpeggios at various dynamic levels and tempos. Keep a steady pulse. Try different articulation patterns, such as:

C Major (Concert B♭ Major)

F Major (Concert E♭ Major)

G Major (Concert F Major)

D Major (Concert C Major)

B♭ Major (Concert A♭ Major)

Eb Major (Concert Db Major)

A Major (Concert G Major)

E Major (Concert D Major)

B Major (Concert A Major)

Ab Major (Concert Gb Major)

Minor Scales

Play minor scales as part of your daily practice routine. Play all octaves, keys, and arpeggios at various dynamic levels and tempos. Keep a steady pulse. Try different articulation patterns, such as:

E Minor (Concert D Minor)

A Minor (Concert G Minor)

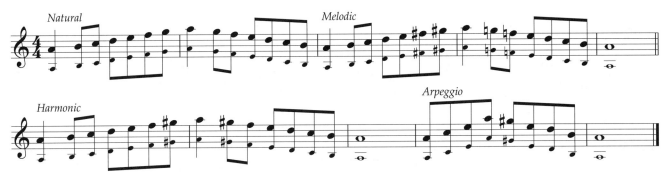

D Minor (Concert C Minor)

G Minor (Concert F Minor)

Vocabulary

Accompaniment music that is secondary, complimentary and supportive to the melodic line

Aeolian a mode beginning and ending on the sixth tone of the major scale, creating the pattern of WHWWHWW (W=whole step/H=half step)

Arpeggiated notes of a chord appearing consecutively in a linear fashion

Cakewalk a strutting dance competition that originated when Southern slaves imitated plantation owners, with the best couple winning a cake

Cantabile in an expressive, singing style

Con with

Countermelody a secondary melodic line set against the primary melody

Counterpoint the combination of two or more melodic lines

Dissonance a disconcerting combination of tones

Dolce sweetly, with tender emotion

Dorian a mode that begins and ends on the second tone of the major scale, creating the pattern of WHWWWHW (W=whole step/ H=half step)

Drone a sustained sound of one or several tones for harmonic support

Duple a rhythmic organization with two beats per measure

Fugato a repeated theme or figure performed in an imitative style

Glissando a smooth ascending or descending slide from one pitch to another

Ground bass a recurring bass line played under changing melodies

Incantation the ritual chanting of magic words

Intermezzo a short piece performed between two longer sections

Inversion (Inverted) the appearance of harmonic or melodic material in a reversed or upside-down order

Legato smooth, graceful, connected

Marcato marked, emphasized, stressed

Mixolydian a mode beginning and ending on the fifth tone of the major scale, creating the pattern of WWHWWHW (W=whole step/H=half step)

Modes a series of ascending or descending whole and half steps arranged to divide the octave into unique patterns

Molto much, very much or extremely

Morendo diminish, fading away

Nationalism musical material that identifies with a specific region, nation or country

Octave interval between two tones seven diatonic pitches apart

Operetta a less serious form of opera that includes spoken dialog songs and dances

Orchestration assigning musical parts to specific instruments in various combinations

Passing tones in a melodic line, non-harmonic tones connecting two harmonic tones using step-wise motion

Pentatonic scale a five-note scale using the first, second, fourth, fifth and sixth tones of a major scale

Perfect 5th two tones, seven half-steps apart, such as the first and fifth tones of a major scale

Pesante heavy, ponderous, weighty

Phrase a musical sentence or complete thought

Phrygian a mode beginning and ending on the third tone of the major scale, creating the pattern of HWWWHWW (W=whole step/H=half step)

Picardy third in the minor mode, the raised third of the final chord

Più more

Pizzicato a string instrument technique where the strings are plucked instead of bowed

Poco little

Polymetric several meters appearing in different parts at the same time

Ragtime an early American jazz style of music using syncopated or "ragged" rhythmic figures

Recapitulation a restatement of the first theme at the ending section of a composition

Resonance a rich ringing sound created through sympathetic vibrations produced when an instrument or ensemble plays with characteristic tone, intonation and balance

Rhapsody (Rhapsodic) an emotional composition featuring irregular form and dramatic style changes

Rubato a hurrying or slowing of the tempo for increased musical expression

Scale a series of ascending or descending notes beginning and ending on a tone of the same letter name

Scherzando playful, lively, animated

Schottische a 19th-century German dance in duple meter performed at a moderate tempo

Semplice simple, plain, pure

Sempre always

Sforzando a sudden stress or emphasis on a single note or chord

Sonority (Sonorous) a deep, rich sound

Sostenuto sustained

Staccatissimo a dry, pointed style

Staccato short, detached, separated

Subito suddenly

Syncopation a rhythmic accent or emphasis on a weak beat or an offbeat

Tenuto held, connected, elongated

Timbre the difference in sound between instruments or voices; tone color

Tonality the organization of a composition around a pitch center

Triple a rhythmic organization with three beats per measure

Tutti an indication for all musicians to play

Unison two or more notes of the same pitch

Vivace lively, fast, brisk

Waltz a dance in triple meter, popular since the late 18th century

Western One-Step a fast ballroom dance that became popular in New York and England around 1910